Scenic
Driving

WISCONSIN

Aaron Cieslicki

FALCON®

HELENA, MONTANA

> *In memory of my father,*
> *Kenneth B. Cieslicki.*

A FALCON GUIDE

Falcon® is continually expanding its list of recreational guidebooks. All books include detailed descriptions, accurate maps, and all the information necessary for enjoyable trips. You can order extra copies of this book and get information and prices for other Falcon® guidebooks by writing Falcon, P.O. Box 1718, Helena, MT 59624 or calling toll-free 1-800-582-2665. Also, please ask for a free copy of our current catalog. To contact us via e-mail, visit our website at http:\\www.falconguide.com.

© 1997 by Falcon® Publishing, Inc., Helena, Montana.
Printed in the United States of America.
10 9 8 7 6 5 4 3 2

All photos by author unless otherwise noted.
Cover photo by Laurance B. Aiuppy.
Back cover photo by Tom Algire.

Cieslicki, Aaron.
    Scenic driving Wisconsin / Aaron Cieslicki.
        p.   cm.
    ISBN 1-56044-558-0 (pbk)
    1. Wisconsin—Tours. 2. Automobile travel—Wisconsin—
    Guidebooks. I. Title.
    F579.3.C54   1997
    917.7504'43—dc21
                                            97-9801
                                            CIP

CAUTION
    All participants in the recreational activities suggested by this book must assume the responsibility for their own actions and safety. The information contained in this guidebook cannot replace sound judgment and good decision-making skills, which help reduce risk exposure; nor does the scope of this book allow for disclosure of all the potential hazards and risks involved in such activities.
    Learn as much as possible about the recreational activities in which you participate, prepare for the unexpected, and be cautious. The reward will be a safer and more enjoyable experience.

Contents

Always go forward, never go straight.

Acknowledgments

There are many people to thank, many people without whom this book would have been a lot less fun and a lot more work. Thanks go to my family, those of blood and those of spirit:

Mom—you always have room no matter what time I call or how short my stay;

My Big Brother, Andy—for going along with my schemes despite your better judgement;

Chuckles the Clown—for balding gracefully (p.s.—the other medical condition will remain our secret);

Marjorie "Never ask a geographer for directions" Rae—for the laughter, and for your relentless attention to detail;

Clan Dana of Goodrich: Nancy—for the welcome, Richard—for keeping the party rolling, Patty—for your boundless energy, Juliet—for keeping me on my toes;

Carrie—navigator, editor, head cheerleader, and all-around bad girl;

Grandpa—for making sure I have enough;

Grandma—for your kitchen table and the family that sits around it;

Aunt Marge—my fairy godmother;

Subie—the meanest, fastest four-wheel-drive grocery-getter in the state;

Ben—for your generous friendship, and your amazing mechanical acumen;

John & Diana—for sharing your cabin in the woods, a great place to write a book.

Locator Map

Map Legend

Scenic Drive (paved)		Interstate	(11)
Scenic Drive (gravel)		U.S. Highway	(11)
Interstate		State Highway	(11)
Other Road		County Road	(Z)
Campground	▲	Forest Service Road	[111]
Hiking Trail		River/Creek	
Map Orientation	N	Lake	
Scale of Miles	0 0.5 1 Mile	Indian Reservation	
Scenic Drive Location		State Park	
		National/State Forest Boundary	
	★	Ranger Station	
		State Boundary	
		Town	○
		Capital	☆

Fall colors on Washington Island. WISCONSIN DEPARTMENT OF TOURISM PHOTO

Introduction

For the record, I was born and raised in Wisconsin (God's Country), so when I wax eloquent about the beauty and virtues of my state you will at least know that I am a Cheesehead. This land of dairy farms and corn, beer and cheese, undying frenzy for the Green Bay Packers, glaciers, blue skies and winding roads is home to Ojibwe, Germans, Czechs, Poles, Winnebago, Finns, Hmong, and Yugoslavs, just to name a few. Wisconsin is a place of widely varying scenes, from towering pines and wild rivers tumbling over waterfalls, to oak and maple-topped rolling hills, to forested lakeshores dotted with lighthouses. The state has almost 2 million acres of state and national forests, excellent hiking, fishing, hunting, canoeing, kayaking, camping, beer drinking, eating, and wildlife viewing. These twenty-four drives will take you around, over, and through the best of it, chasing glaciers and following rivers, along forest roads and rural highways, as well as into some of the cities across the state. Some of the routes stick to one highway, and some take four or five, following the shape of the land.

There are many different stories about the origin of the name Wisconsin, and many of them agree that the state takes its name from its largest river, the Wisconsin. The one I like best says that it derives from the Ojibwe word that French explorer Father Hennepin wrote as *Ouisconsing*, meaning "gathering of the waters," when he named the state's major river on his map. James Doty, an influential judge and politician, is said to have insisted in the 1830s that the name derives from the Winnebago term for the Wisconsin River, *Wees-koos-erah*, meaning "river of the flowing banks" (or, less poetically, "the river"). The Wisconsin River starts at Lac Vieux Desert, a lake that straddles the border between Wisconsin and the Upper Peninsula of Michigan, runs south through the center of the state, and finally empties into the Mississippi River at Prairie du Chien in southwestern Wisconsin. Along its banks you'll find much of Wisconsin's history—camps and portages, council grounds, saw mills, inns, forts, and paper mills.

Wisconsin's northernmost lands border Lake Superior, the world's largest freshwater lake. The Apostle Islands National Lakeshore on Lake Superior's south shore (Drive 10) is perhaps the most raved-about scenery in the state. The Apostle Islands National Lakeshore protects pine-topped red cliffs along 12 miles of mainland shore and 21 forested and rocky outlying islands. You'll be tempted to park your car and get on a boat to explore the caves and occasional beaches of the islands—through the misty dawn they look close enough to touch from the mainland.

People have been enjoying the summers in Door County (Drive 3) in eastern Wisconsin for two thousand years—an archaeological dig at Whitefish Dunes State Park unearthed evidence that groups had used the area as summer hunting and fishing grounds as early as 100 B.C. Door County comprises the northern end of the Door Peninsula, which sticks out into Lake Michigan (Wisconsin's other Great Lake) and separates Green Bay from the big lake. Dotted with orchards and farms, and five state parks, the county is mostly shoreline, with white limestone cliffs on the Green Bay side and wide, sandy beaches on the Lake Michigan side. Off the tip of the peninsula, Washington and Rock Islands offer forested seclusion for the cost of a ferry ride across Porte des Mortes—"Death's Door" to French fur traders in canoes—known for its sometimes stormy passage.

The northern half of the state is given over to forests and lakes and rivers. In the northeast, the Northern Highlands are a series of hills that were a mountain range as high and jagged as the Rockies several million years ago. The drives through the north country cross the Nicolet and Chequamegon National Forests, as well as the Northern Highland American Legion and the Brule River State Forests. You'll find waterfalls, great blue heron rookeries, pineries, iron mines, hundreds of lakes, fishing, hiking, camping, and plenty of solitude, if that's what you like.

Southern Wisconsin is more populous than the northern half of the state, partly because the land is better suited to agriculture, and partly because Milwaukee, now the state's largest city, was the chief port of entry for Wisconsin's settlers. The countryside is devoted to mostly dairy farming and corn, with some soy beans, potatoes, beef cattle, and cranberry bogs thrown in as well. Southern Wisconsin has three state forests: Point Beach State Forest on the Lake Michigan shore, Kettle Moraine State Forest in the southeast, and Black River State Forest in the west. You're never far from a cheese factory in the southern part of the state, or a cold glass of beer for that matter. The south is a mixture of prairies, wetlands, and upland forests of both pines and hardwoods.

Before you go

Wisconsin's state parks and forests boast a total of more than five thousand campsites, and on a summer weekend it can seem like all of the sites are taken. If you're planning to camp as you go, there are a few tactics for securing a site. First, you can reserve a campsite using the Wisconsin Department of Natural Resources (DNR) campsite registration form—you can get one by contacting the DNR at the location listed in the appendix. This works well if you're planning your itinerary in advance. Second, you can call ahead to reserve a site—telephone numbers for state parks and forests are listed by drive number in the appendix. If there are no spots left open to reserve, you can still sometimes get a state park site by showing up at the park office before 10 A.M. Most state park campgrounds have a certain number of sites set aside that can't be reserved—these are assigned on a first come, first serve basis at 10 A.M. The sooner you get there, the better your chances are of getting a site. In the Chequamegon and Nicolet National Forests, you can camp anywhere in the general forest area as long as you're at least 50 feet from lakes, streams, trails, and roads. There are also innumerable private campgrounds (including the irrepressible KOAs) in every part of the state.

All of the drives in this book travel the back roads for at least a few miles. During winter these roads are often covered with a layer of ice and snow—slow and easy, cowboy. All year round the chief obstacle on these roads is the deer. They are most active (and most likely to dive beneath your bumper) in the hours around dusk and dawn, though sometimes you'll see them along the highway during the day.

Glacial history

One summer about a million years ago, way up in northern Canada, it was so cold that not all of the snow that fell the previous winter melted. This was but the beginning of the cold snap—summer after summer the cold continued, and the snow built higher and higher. Eventually, after thousands of years, the snow at the bottom of the immense pile was compacted into ice from the weight of the snow above it. Then, physicists say, the ice at the bottom of the snow pile began to actually flow like a liquid. The pile of snow turned into a glacier. The glacier became ambulatory and headed south. It eventually covered most of North America east of the Rockies, only to recede and then advance again.

Geologists have identified four major waves of glaciation during the Ice Age that occurred from one million to ten thousand years ago. The last wave of glaciation in the Ice Age started about twenty-five thousand years ago and ended ten thousand years ago, covering an area from Montana to New York, and most of Wisconsin. This final glacial wave is called Wisconsin Glaciation. Geologists have found some of the best-preserved geological records of the glacier's passing here. When you read or hear about Wisconsin's glacial history, it is usually only this last wave of glaciation that is being discussed.

As the glacier scraped south from Canada, it did not advance as a single unit—variations in local topography caused different sections to advance at different rates. Eastern Wisconsin was completely glaciated, as was northern Wisconsin. Curiously, though, the southwest corner of the state escaped the ravages of the glacier, and is known today as the Driftless Area—a rolling upland deeply cut by a maze of interconnecting river valleys (Drives 15, 17, and 18).

The glacier was an amazing earth-moving force. As it flowed and bulldozed its way across the land, it sheared off the tops of hills, scraped up sand and gravel, and picked up boulders. This material was carried along the front edge of the glacier, sometimes for hundreds of miles. When the glacier began to melt about twelve thousand years ago, the debris riding the front of the glacier dropped to the ground, leaving long lines of hills, called moraines, which mark the farthest extent of the glacier's reach. The Ice Age National Scenic Trail follows the meandering moraines across the state, wandering 1,000 miles from its eastern end in Door County to its western end at Interstate State Park on the St. Croix River.

The torrents of rushing water from the melting glacier shaped the land in several distinct ways, creating kames (conical hills), eskers (long, sinuous hills), and outwash plains (broad, flat, sandy plains). The retreating glacier also left kettles (bowl-shaped depressions) and drumlins (hills that some say look like whales). In southern Wisconsin, near Wisconsin Dells, a moraine blocked the Wisconsin River Valley. As ice became water in the glacier's melting, the meltwater backed up behind the blockage, creating a huge lake called Glacial Lake Wisconsin (Drives 21 and 22). The Kettle Moraine Scenic Drive (Drive 1) follows the Kettle Moraine from north to south and shows off the state's best collection of glacial landforms. The Chippewa Moraine (Drive 24) marks the farthest southward extent of the glacier in north central Wisconsin, with lakes in many of the numerous kettles. The moraine in the south (Drive 19) sits atop Driftless Area hills, and is fairly dry, with few lakes.

By about ten thousand years ago, the glacier had disappeared from the state, and left behind huge quantities of water. Wisconsin's human history begins with the close of the Ice Age.

Human history

The earliest evidence of human habitation in Wisconsin was found under a rock shelter at Natural Bridge State Park (Drive 17). The artifacts collected there date back about twelve thousand years, to the time when the glacier was beginning to melt back northward. Various peoples moved through the region for thousands of years, and of most of them history has no record. Two ancient peoples, however, have left us their legacies: the Old Copper Culture Indians and the Effigy Mound Builders.

The Old Copper Culture Indians flourished in northern and northeastern Wisconsin from about 5000 B.C. to around 500 B.C. They often lived near copper deposits, which they mined for the ore to make weapons, tools, and adornment. Most of what is known about them comes from those of their implements which have survived to the present day—the subtleties of their culture remain a mystery. In the mines the Copper Culture worked thousands of years ago, archaeologists have found stone hammers, copper chisels, copper knives, copper spear points, and pieces of charcoal. The veins they mined can be found today at Pattison and Amincon Falls State Parks (Drive 10). The summer camp of at least one group of the Copper Culture Indians was located at present-day Peninsula State Park (Drive 3), and a

Kayaking in the Apostle Islands. WISCONSIN DEPARTMENT OF TOURISM PHOTO

Copper Culture burial mound is the centerpiece of Copper Culture Mound State Park (Drive 4).

The Effigy Mound Builders, who appeared sometime after 1000 B.C., left their bas-relief markers in several parts of the state. Wyalusing State Park (Drives 16 and 17) is home to a fantastic collection of twenty-five mounds. The mounds (10 to 15 feet high and up to 60 feet long) are sculpted into the shapes of foxes, deer, bears, lizards, buffalo, and crosses, as well as some conical mounds, which were used as burial mounds. One archaeologist in the late 1800s reportedly found seven skeletons in one of the conical mounds, facing east in a sitting position.

Whatever the significance of the effigy mounds to their builders—art? religion? both? neither?—that meaning is lost to the recesses of time. The mounds had some significance to the peoples that came after the Effigy Mound Builders as well—graves of more recent origin than the mounds themselves have been found atop many of the effigy mounds near Madison.

Between the demise of the Effigy Mound Builders and the arrival of French explorers in 1634, several peoples called Wisconsin home, for a short time, at least, either chasing or being chased by their enemies, in search of new lands. The Ojibwe were driven from their homes in the St. Lawrence River Valley to Madeline Island on Lake Superior (Drive 10) by the

Algonquins about the time of Columbus's first visit to the New World. The Sauk tradition holds that the Sauk tribe originally hailed from the Montreal area, but was driven first to Mackinaw in Michigan and then farther west to Green Bay, where they met and allied themselves with the Fox. The ancient enemy of the Sauk continued to pursue them, and the Sauk and the Fox, now united as one people, traveled west and made two settlements, one near present-day Sauk City on the Wisconsin River, and one at the mouth of the Rock River in the Mississippi River Valley. Other groups in the area included the Dakota, Winnebago, Potowatomi, Menominee, Huron, Ottawa, and Kickapoo, among others.

Jean Nicolet was on a mission in 1634 to push deep into the northwest and establish the fur trade for New France when he landed with his company of *voyageurs* near present-day Green Bay. He stepped from his canoe in a flowing Oriental robe (he thought he would be landing in the Orient) and fired off two pistols, making a great impression on the Winnebago and other tribes that met him. After a series of feasts they agreed to engage in fur trade, made a pact of peace, and Nicolet returned to Lake Huron to make his report.

In 1659, the French explorers Radisson and Groseilliers reached the Mississippi River (Drives 14 and 16), and in 1661 the two explored the south shore of Lake Superior (Drive 10) before traveling inland to Hayward (Drives 9 and 11) to establish trade with the Ojibwe. More explorers followed, establishing fur trade with the tribes they met. The French, interested primarily in the fur trade, had no intention to settle the northwest. They were content to have a small number of agents trade manufactured goods such as muskets, axes, knives, blankets, cookware, and wine to the local tribes for furs, chiefly beaver. By 1700, when the British colonies to the east had roughly 250,000 inhabitants, the European population of New France totaled 20,000. These numbers proved decisive in the ensuing struggle for control of North America.

In 1763, Wisconsin became British territory. France, defeated by Britain in the Seven Years War, ceded Canada and all lands east of the Mississippi to the British. At that time, British settlement of the continent from the east reached only to the foothills of the Appalachian Mountains. The British actively discouraged settlement of the region in an attempt to mollify tribes angry at European expansion, and continued the trade-only policy of the French. The fur trade, centered in Montreal, continued much as it had before.

Only the last years of the Revolutionary War disrupted the fur trade. When Wisconsin became U.S. territory in 1783 the trade resumed, though it continued to be dominated by the British. Despite ceding the land to the new United States of America in the treaty of 1783, British troops still controlled the lands west of the Appalachians. A treaty signed in 1794 gave

British traders the same advantages as Americans, and life in Wisconsin remained little changed. It wasn't until 1815, at the end of the War of 1812, that the U.S. finally managed to kick the British out of Wisconsin.

Settlement began in earnest in 1826, when the discovery of lead near Mineral Point (Drive 18), in the southwestern part of the state, attracted four thousand settlers. At the same time, immigrants began arriving in Milwaukee as the U.S. population surged toward the Mississippi. While the British recognized U.S. title to the land, the region's native tribes did not, and were little pleased with the lead rush that brought settlers. In 1827, Chief Red Bird and a group of Winnebago prepared for war to drive the intruders out, though they surrendered when surrounded by the U.S. Army and local militia. Soon after, the Winnebago, Ojibwe, Ottawa, and Potowatomi ceded all of southern Wisconsin to the United States. Northern Wisconsin soon followed.

Loggers moved into the Wisconsin, Black, Chippewa, and St. Croix River valleys and began cutting the vast stands of white pine that covered the area. Settlers flowed through Milwaukee and started farming wheat on the newly-cleared land. Towns grew up on rivers around flour mills and lumber mills, which used rivers to turn millstones and saw blades. Wisconsin joined the Union as the thirtieth state in 1848, and by 1850 the population was nearly 300,000. By the turn of the century the seemingly inexhaustible forests of white pine were gone, and loggers turned their attention to the upland hardwood forests. The hardwoods had remained largely untouched because they wouldn't float downriver like pine; now lumber barons became railroad builders, laying down hundreds of miles of track to ship the hardwoods from the forests to the mills.

Farmers continued to follow loggers north toward Lake Superior after the turn of the century, but the farmers soon discovered that the cutover northern lands that once supported vast forests were not especially good cropland. Most of the northern farms failed and were abandoned during the farm depression of the 1920s and the Great Depression of the 1930s. Someone suggested that if crops wouldn't grow in the north, maybe the trees could be replanted. That they were: Chequamegon National Forest was established in 1933, and numerous state and county forests were established across the northern half of the state in the 1930s, all with the mission of replanting trees and managing timber as a renewable resource.

Architect Frank Lloyd Wright was born in Richland Center in 1867, and in 1911, Wright returned to Wisconsin to build his home, Taliesin, near Spring Green (Drive 17). From 1911 to 1956, Wright worked on his home and other commissions. The architecture of southern Wisconsin has been much enhanced by his work and that of his students.

During the Great Depression, the Civilian Conservation Corps (CCC) was created as a jobs program by the Roosevelt administration. CCC workers built dikes to restore wetlands, planted trees in the northern forests, and helped develop state parks, building campgrounds and trails. In the 1950s, Wisconsin Senator Joseph McCarthy made headaches for the nation as chief instigator of the Red Scare. The 1970s saw the most recent wave of immigration to the state—the Hmong people from the mountains of Laos, who were U.S. allies during the Vietnam War. Today, Wisconsin is America's Dairy State, a place of forests and fields, trout streams, and Great Lakes. Welcome to Wisconsin!

1

Kettle Moraine Scenic Drive

Kettle Moraine State Forest

General description: This 115-mile drive follows the Kettle Moraine, a long ridge of forested hills that mark where two great arms of the last glacier butted up against each other. The route follows the Kettle Moraine Scenic Drive developed and maintained by the Kettle Moraine State Forest staff. Along the way you're likely to learn more about glacial geology than you ever thought you'd know. You will travel many unmarked back roads on this route (peek at the drive route numbers below), wandering all over hell and creation in search of yet more glacial formations to gawk at, and it is likely to fill an enjoyable day of driving.

Special attractions: Kettle Moraine State Forest, glacial geology, hiking, biking, camping, cross-country skiing, fishing.

Location: Southeastern Wisconsin, starting west of Sheboygan and ending southwest of Milwaukee.

Drive route numbers: Wisconsin Highways 23, 33, 59, 60, 67, 144, 167, U.S. Highway 45, Sheboygan County Highways A, F, G, S, U, V, SS, GGG, Jefferson County Highway H, Washington County Highways E and K, Waukesha County Highways C, E, G, K, GG, VV, Kettle Moraine Drive, Clover Valley Road, Engle Road.

Travel season: Year-round.

Camping: Mauthe Lake Recreation Area, Long Lake Recreation Area, Pine Woods Campground, Ottawa Lake Recreation Area, Whitewater Lake Recreation Area.

Services: Limited services along the entire route.

 The drive

Around twenty-five thousand years ago, the last great wave of the Ice Age glaciers was storming south from the Upper Peninsula of Michigan with a good head of steam (for a glacier) when it ran into Door County (Drive 3), north of the start of this drive. A glacier is fairly sensitive to the topography it runs up against, and when the last glacier hit the rocky peninsula we know as Door County, it split into two arms (called lobes by

9

glaciologists), and each continued south. The Kettle Moraine (properly called an interlobate moraine) is the line of hills made up of piled-up glacial sediment that was deposited where these two lobes abutted, and contains some of the best examples of glacial landforms from the last Ice Age to be found in the world.

It seems like many of the roads on this route wouldn't have been paved if the state forest hadn't developed the Kettle Moraine Scenic Drive route. Many of the intersections and roads are unmarked, so watch for the green Kettle Moraine Scenic Drive signs that mark most of the route.

The drive begins at the intersection of Wisconsin Highway 23 and Sheboygan County A, in the town of Greenbush. From WI 23, turn south onto County A. You'll soon find the Wade House, which, when completed in 1853 by Sylvanus Wade, became the most important stagecoach stop on the plank road running from Sheboygan to Fond du Lac. The historical complex here includes a blacksmith shop where horses were shod and stages repaired, as well as the Butternut House, home to Wade's eldest daughter and son-in-law.

At the stop sign with the Wade House on the right, turn right. One block later, turn left, and then right after another block. After a short distance, take another left, following the Kettle Moraine Scenic Drive signs. The road here is winding and narrow, and the trees close in on either side as you bump over the moraine. You'll pass the Greenbush Recreation Area and Greenbush Picnic Area (great spots for hiking and mountain biking) before you come to the second stop on this tour, Greenbush Kettle.

The parking area for Greenbush Kettle is on the left, just past a sign that says "Shelter 5." Park and walk back along the entrance road to a trail and a wooden stairway leading down into a big hole in the earth—Greenbush Kettle. Standing at the lip of the kettle, imagine being here ten thousand years ago, at the end of the Ice Age. The glacier has mostly retreated to north of here, and there is no hole before you, just a treeless space covered with sand and boulders. Beneath the sand at this spot is a huge piece of ice left behind in the glacier's retreat. As time passed, the ice melted and the land dropped, finally leaving this depression. You can best appreciate the immensity of the stranded ice chunk from the bottom of the stairs.

Just past Greenbush Kettle, the road forks. Follow Kettle Moraine Scenic Drive to the right. At the stop sign and junction with Wisconsin Highway 67, turn left onto WI 67. Travel approximately 0.5 mile to County A and turn right. The mixed pine and hardwood forest here is dense, and the road rolls up and down through the moraine. At the junction with Sheboygan County U, turn right and travel approximately 0.25 mile to the parking area for Parnell Tower, a 50-foot observation tower built atop a high ridge of the moraine. The tower is about an eighth of a mile up the trail leading from the parking lot. The view from the tower is well worth the

Drive 1: Kettle Moraine Scenic Drive

Kettle Moraine State Forest

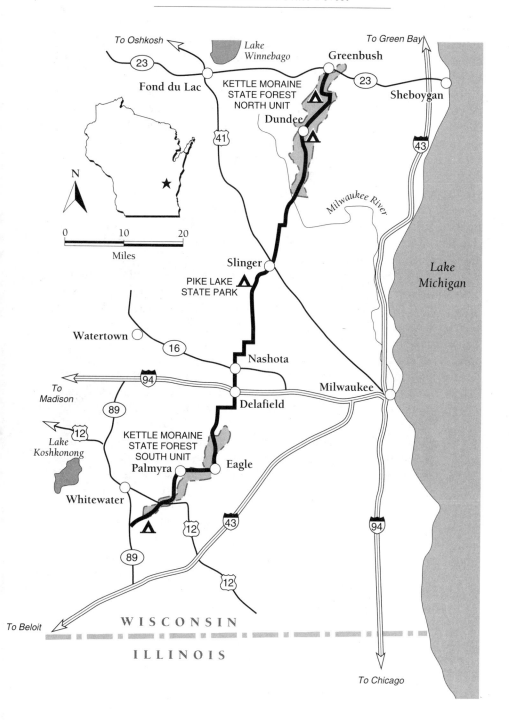

climb. To the west, in the distance, you'll see a series of bumps that rise above the relatively flat land around them. These are drumlins, glacial debris composed mainly of silt and clay with some small pebbles. The long axis of the drumlin is arranged in the direction of the ice's forward movement, roughly north-south here.

Turn right onto County U out of the Parnell Tower parking area, travel just over 1 mile and turn left onto Woodside Road/Kettle Moraine Drive. After traveling 0.25 mile, turn left onto Shamrock Road; go 0.25 mile further and turn left onto the Scenic Drive. At the next stop sign you come to, turn left onto Sheboygan County V (though the road isn't marked at the intersection), and then after a short distance on County V, turn left (following the Kettle Moraine Scenic Drive sign) onto Butler Lake Road. The long sinuous ridge on the left side of the road is the Parnell Esker, one of the longer eskers in the state forest. Eskers mark the path of meltwater streams that flowed underneath the ice and consist of the glacial sediment deposited along the bed of the sub-glacial stream.

At the stop sign, turn left, and at the next stop sign and the junction with Sheboygan County F, turn right. At the next stop sign and the intersection with WI 67 in downtown Dundee, go forward, following WI 67 south. Dundee is home to the world-famous (among geology buffs, anyway) Dundee Kame, known locally as Dundee Mountain, a 250-foot pile of sand, pebbles, and boulders that formed at the bottom of a hole in the retreating glacier. Glacial meltwater streams running along the glacier's surface washed the debris into the hole, and the debris accumulated at the bottom of the hole. The perimeter of the base of the Kame will give you an idea of the size of the hole in the ice.

For a good view of Dundee Kame and more glacial geology, head for the Henry S. Reuss Ice Age Visitor Center up a hill just outside of Dundee on WI 67. As you're headed up the hill, you'll notice that the Kettle Moraine Scenic Drive veers off to the left on Sheboygan County G. If you want to skip the interpretive center, follow it left here. Otherwise, continue up the hill to the top and turn left into the center's driveway. The center features a large mural depicting the surrounding area roughly ten to twelve thousand years ago, at the time of the glacier's final retreat. The center shows a twenty minute film, and signs outside the center interpret several glacial features visible nearby.

When you leave the center, turn right onto WI 67 and then right again onto County G and the Kettle Moraine Scenic Drive route. After rolling through the forest a bit, the road drops down to run alongside a glacial outwash terrace. A restored prairie now covers the outwash terrace. The terrace formed when sand and gravel were washed by meltwater streams from the retreating glacier's surface and deposited here, forming this broad, flat plain. At the intersection with Sheboygan County SS, turn left and cross

Old World Wisconsin, composed of actual farmhouses, barns, and village shops built by pioneer immigrants. WISCONSIN DEPARTMENT OF TOURISM PHOTO

the outwash terrace. There is a wildlife viewing area on the left side of the road not far from the intersection. When you've crossed to the other side of the terrace, turn right onto Sheboygan County GGG.

This paragraph is devoted entirely to directions to get you through an extremely poorly marked section of this route. Stay sharp. Here goes. When county GGG meets Sheboygan County S, turn right, and at the stop sign in New Fane, turn left. After going forward through a couple of intersections, turn right at the T-intersection (which was completely devoid of signs or markings when I was here). At the next stop sign, turn right and cross the Milwaukee River. At the stop sign across the river, go forward, and at the stop sign and intersection with U.S. Highway 45, turn right onto US 45 south. You'll go up a big hill, and at the top of the hill turn left. Go forward at the next stop sign, and at the stop sign after that turn right.

If all is well, the next intersection you come to should be Glacier Drive, where you turn right. At the intersection with Wisconsin Highways 33 and 144, follow WI 144 south. You have now left the North Unit of the Kettle Moraine State Forest. WI 144 runs along the top of the moraine, with wooded hills all around. At the stop sign in the town of Slinger, go forward. Turn right at the junction with Wisconsin Highway 60 onto WI 60 west, and after approximately 2 miles turn left into Pike Lake State Park on Kettle Moraine

Road. Pike Lake State Park has twenty-five well-spaced campsites, as well as hiking, biking, fishing, and swimming. The park office is on the left at the WI 60/Kettle Moraine Drive intersection, and Pike Lake is just over the hill on the left.

Continue on Kettle Moraine Drive past the intersection with Washington County E, and at the intersection with Waterford Road, turn right. At the junction with Washington County K, turn left. On your left, just after you turn onto County K, is Holy Hill (a kame, actually), the highest point in the Kettle Moraine and the site of a Catholic monastery. An observation deck at the top of the hill provides spectacular views of the surrounding countryside. To get to Holy Hill, turn left onto WI 167 and follow it up the hill. Otherwise, keep headed south on County K, which, when it reaches the county line, changes (in name only) to Waukesha County E.

The next town you come to is Monches, named for an Indian chief who lived near here. Just after Monches, County E turns right at a stop sign. Follow it, and then at the intersection with Waukesha County VV, turn right. In the town of North Lake, turn left onto Wisconsin Highway 83 at the stop sign. At the intersection with Waukesha County K, turn right onto County K. After a few miles, turn left onto Waukesha County C. You'll cross over Wisconsin Highway 16 at Neshota, one of the far outposts of the Milwaukee metro area. Continue on County C to Delafield, home of the Fox Inn, once an important stopping point on the stagecoach route that ran between Madison and Milwaukee. In Delafield, turn right onto Wells Street/County C, and you'll see the Fox Inn from the road.

Outside of Delafield, County C crosses I-94, and on the left after you cross the interstate is Lapham Peak, birthplace of the National Weather Service. Increase A. Lapham, a conservationist and scientist who lived here in the 1800s (also winner of the Goofy Name Award and the peak's namesake), worked with the U.S. Army Signal Corps to set up a series of signal stations between Pike's Peak in Colorado and Lapham Peak to transmit weather data from west to east. Blue Mound State Park (Drive 19) west of Madison was the site of one of the stations. The meteorological data was transmitted to Lapham's office in Chicago, and Lapham then warned Great Lakes ports of impending storms. The view from the peak is excellent, showing sixteen of the surrounding lakes.

At the stop sign after Lapham Peak, follow County C to the right. After approximately 1 mile, follow County C when it turns left. At the intersection with Waukesha County G, you'll cross what was once an important Indian trail running from Lake Koshkonng (west of Whitewater) to Milwaukee. Don't worry if you don't actually see the trail; it's not marked. Turn right here and follow County C.

At the intersection with Waukesha County D, cross County D and immediately turn left onto Town G/Waterville Road. At the fork in the road and the sign for County GG, bear right. At the next intersection, turn right to enter the South Unit of the Kettle Moraine State Forest. At the junction with WI 67, turn left onto WI 67, and in a few miles you come to Eagle, where the first diamond found in Wisconsin was discovered in 1876. Eagle is also home to Old World Wisconsin, a collection of more than 50 historic farmhouses, barns, and merchant shops on 600 acres of wooded hills. If you'd like to see it, follow WI 67 approximately 3 miles south of town. If not, take Wisconsin Highway 59, the right-most road at the funky six-way intersection in Eagle.

In Palmyra, approximately 6 miles out of Eagle, go forward onto Jefferson County H where WI 59 turns right. On your right, a short way down County H, you'll see cropland in a shallow valley. The land surrounding the valley is a glacial outwash plain, created when fine glacial particles were washed out of the glacier by running water. The valley itself is called a spillway, where a smaller meltwater stream cut through the already-deposited sandy plain. Turn right onto Kettle Moraine Drive, cross the spillway, and roll through the outwash plain. The wooded ridge on your right is the moraine you've been following this whole drive. On the left side of the road you can see (provided the corn isn't too high) the Elkhorn Recessional Moraine in the far distance. The glacier's progress, both advancing and retreating, was erratic; in the major advance of the last wave of glaciation from twenty-five thousand to fifteen thousand years ago, there were many retreats. This moraine marks the spot of a significant pause in the final retreat of the Lake Michigan Lobe of the glacier.

Go forward at the next stop sign, and the stop sign after that, and you come to the Whitewater Recreation Area, with sixty-four campsites, a picnic area, a beach, and a boat landing. Drive 0.75 mile past the recreation area and turn right onto Clover Valley Road. At the intersection with Engle Road a mile later, turn right and travel 0.2 mile to the end of this drive, where there is a hand-dug artesian well that has been flowing steadily since 1895. The water is clear, clean, cold, and extremely refreshing for weary travelers on a hot day.

To get back to civilization, travel back to Kettle Moraine Drive, turn right, and follow it to Wisconsin Highway 89. A right onto WI 89 will take you to Whitewater and U.S. Highway 12.

2

Lake Michigan
Sand Dunes and Submarines

General description: This drive tours the Lake Michigan shore from Sheboygan to Algoma, passing sand dunes, high bluffs, lighthouses, farms, and museums. The area's flavor and history are closely tied to the lake through fishing, sailing, and ship building.
Special attractions: Kohler-Andrae State Park, Point Beach State Forest, the USS *Cobia*, lighthouses, museums, hiking, swimming, fishing, camping, wildlife watching.
Location: Southeastern Wisconsin. The drive begins at Kohler-Andrae State Park and ends in Algoma.
Drive route numbers: Interstate Highway 43, Sheboygan County V, Wisconsin Highways 23 and 42, Sheboygan and Manitowoc County Highway LS, Manitowoc County Highways O and V.
Travel season: Year-round.
Camping: Kohler-Andrae State Park and Point Beach State Forest.
Services: Full services in Sheboygan and Manitowoc, limited elsewhere.

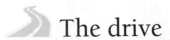 The drive

This 90-mile drive starts at Kohler-Andrae State Park, a few miles south of Sheboygan. From Interstate Highway 43, turn east onto Sheboygan County Highway V, then right onto Sheboygan County Highway KK, and then left onto Old Park Road to the park entrance. The park's landscape is a mix of river marsh, pine and hardwood forests, beaches, and sand dunes. Creeping Juniper and Woodland Dunes nature trails will take you through the forest and sand dunes near the lakeshore, and the 2.5 mile Kohler Dunes Cordwalk runs parallel to the lakeshore and through a State Natural Area. The 1,000 acre park has 105 campsites, a swimming beach, and a nature center with displays on local flora, fauna, and history.

Travel back to I-43 and take it north toward Sheboygan. After 6 miles on I-43, take Wisconsin Highway 23 east into Sheboygan. Jacques Vieau established a Northwest Fur Company post here in 1795, to trade with the Ottawa and Ojibwe Indians who inhabited the area. The first white settlers in the area were David Wilson and his family, who came here from New

Drive 2: Lake Michigan
Sand Dunes and Submarines

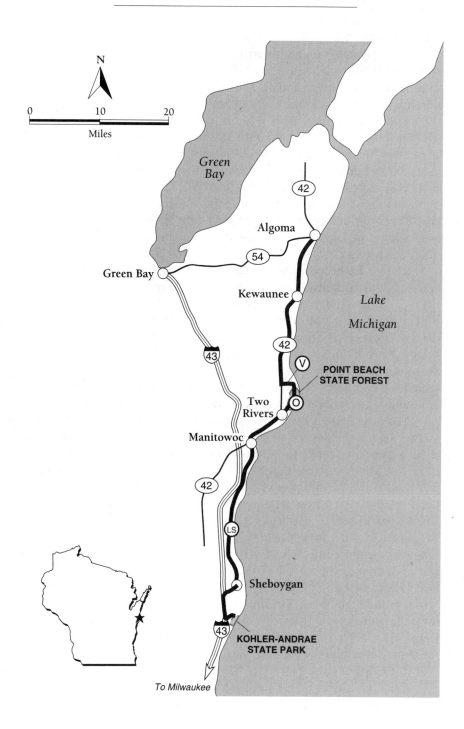

York in 1840, followed by brothers James and Leonard Osgood who arrived in 1845. The men set up fisheries, and all three drowned in the icy waters of Lake Michigan while plying their trade. From the 1850s to the 1870s, German and Dutch immigrants arrived to farm the land east of the lake. The Sheboygan County Museum, on Erie Avenue, boasts an 1864 log house, antique farm machinery, and an 1867 cheese factory, in addition to a mansion full of late-nineteenth-century items.

At the intersection with Wisconsin Highway 42 in Sheboygan, turn left onto WI 42, and then right onto Sheboygan County Highway LS a mile or so later. Just out of town, LS rolls along near the top of a bluff and past miles of sand dunes from Sheboygan to the Manitowoc County line. Two miles past the county line, near the town of Cleveland, County LS takes a right, and then bends around again to the left to continue along the shoreline. The farms on this stretch are plowed right to the edge of the steep bluff overlooking the lake, and from the right angle it appears the tractors are tilling the waves.

County LS becomes South 10th Street when you enter Manitowoc. Follow South 10th Street, and turn left onto Maritime Drive immediately after you cross the river. Manitowoc was built on shipbuilding. The Wisconsin Maritime Museum at 75 Maritime Drive exhibits one hundred years of Great Lakes history. The USS *Cobia*, one of twenty-eight U.S. Navy submarines built in Manitowoc during World War II, is moored adjacent to the museum. The *Cobia* is open for daily tours year-round, and in the museum itself two floors of yachts, freighters, sailboats, steamers, and a seven-thousand-volume library of Upper Midwest history await you.

Maritime Drive is also WI 42, so continue north on it out of Manitowoc to Two Rivers, 6 miles away. The East and West Twin Rivers join up here about a quarter of a mile from Lake Michigan and flow into the lake as one river. Just after you cross the West Twin River, a right on 16th Street will take you to the Washington House Museum, housed in what was once a hotel. It's said that Ed Berners invented the ice cream sundae right here in Two Rivers, in 1881. A replica of his ice cream parlor offers eighteen different sundaes, and you can take in local history displays in the other five rooms of the museum. Back at WI 42, the route turns right on 22nd Street and then crosses the East Twin River. A right at the first street (Jackson Street) across the river, takes you to the Rogers Street Fishing Village Museum and Lighthouse. The museum houses displays on commercial fishing, telling the story of the French-Canadian fishermen who settled here in Deux Rivers. There are also exhibits about Coast Guard history. The museum is listed on the National Register of Historic Places and is open all year; the lighthouse is open from April to November.

On 22nd Street, WI 42 turns left 2.5 blocks from the river. Continue on 22nd Street for 3 blocks and then turn left onto Manitowoc County High-

Shore of Lake Michigan along Point Beach State Forest.

way O. County O (a.k.a. Wisconsin Department of Transportation Rustic Road R-16) is 5 miles of highway bordered on both sides by thick groves of hardwoods and pines, offers great views of sand dunes and local wildlife, and leads to Point Beach State Forest. The forest features beautiful trees, 6 miles of sandy beach, 12 miles of hiking, and 127 campsites. The forest is also home to Rawley Point Lighthouse, which has been operated since 1853 by the U.S. Coast Guard. The lighthouse was a brick tower until 1894, when a 113-foot steel tower was built, and the old tower chopped down, roofed, and used as part of the lighthouse keeper's residence. The light mounted atop the tower is visible up to 19 miles away and operates today from one-half hour before sunset to one-half hour after sunrise.

County O ends just beyond the northern border of the state forest, and the road becomes Manitowoc County Highway V as you follow it to the left. Follow this approximately 3 miles back to WI 42 and turn right. From here to Kewaunee, 15 miles north, the land is sparsely settled, with bluff-hugging farms interspersed with stand of trees. In Kewaunee, architecture lovers will enjoy the variety of house styles from the late nineteenth and twentieth centuries, including Queen Anne, Italianate, Second Empire, Craftsman, Prairie and American Foursquare styles. The Kewaunee Chamber of Commerce publishes a walking-tour booklet that provides a map of

Fast sailing on Lake Michigan. WISCONSIN DEPARTMENT OF TOURISM PHOTO

forty historic homes.

Algoma is the end of this drive, 11 miles north of Kewaunee on WI 42. Algoma is also home to the southern end of the Ahnapee State Trail, the 15-mile state trail running from Algoma to Sturgeon Bay, which forms the first (or last) segment of the Ice Age National Scenic Trail. The Ice Age Trail follows the moraines left by the glaciers across Wisconsin.

From Algoma, Wisconsin Highway 54 will take you to Green Bay and the start of Drive 3.

3

Door County
State Parks and Shoreline

General description: More than 250 miles of shoreline dotted with light-houses and 40 islands await you on this 130-mile drive through Door County. Limestone bluffs, rocky shores, dairy farms, cherry and apple orchards, and five state parks, including the state's largest park, Peninsula State Park, are found along the Door Peninsula. One of Wisconsin's most scenic places, the summer camping, fishing, hiking, boating, and swimming on the shores of Green Bay and Lake Michigan have been a tradition for over two thousand years.

Special attractions: Lambeau Field, Green Bay Packer Hall of Fame, Potawatomi State Park, Peninsula State Park, Newport State Park, Rock Island State Park, Whitefish Dunes State Park, cherry pie, hiking, mountain biking, swimming, fishing, boating, camping.

Location: Eastern Wisconsin, beginning in Green Bay and ending at White-fish Dunes State Park.

Drive route numbers: Wisconsin Highways 57 and 42, Door County Highways BB, B, G, W, NP and WD.

Travel season: Year-round. High season runs from early July to late August.

Camping: 125 sites at Potawatomi State Park, 469 sites at Peninsula State Park, 16 backpack-only sites at Newport State Park, 30 campground and 5 backpack-only sites at Rock Island State Park, several private campgrounds. Reservations recommended for campsites during high season.

Services: Full services in Green Bay and Sturgeon Bay, limited elsewhere.

 The drive

The drive begins in Green Bay, Wisconsin's earliest European settle-ment. In 1634, French explorer Jean Nicolet was the first European to travel to Wisconsin. He waded to shore near here and made a treaty establishing the fur trade with the Winnebago, Potawatomi, and other tribes gathered around the mouth of the Fox River. It was more than twenty years before any traders made their way back. In 1669 a Jesuit priest named Father Allouez established a mission here, and in 1680, France built a fortified post manned by a small detachment of soldiers. For a while, Green Bay was the base of operations for the French army as they fought with the tribes that opposed them. The French maintained a trade-only policy in regard to the people and lands here, and settlement was not a priority—in 1745 the settlement's population totaled eight souls. By 1812, the land was U.S. territory and the poulation stood at 250. Green Bay grew as a trading, shipping, and rail center. The Neville Public Museum's 7,500-square-foot "On the Edge of the Inland Sea" exhibit at 210 Museum Place chronicles local history from the end of the Ice Age twelve thousand years ago, to the twentieth century. It's open daily until 4 P.M. The National Railroad Museum, open daily from 9 A.M. to 5 P.M., at 2285 South Broadway Avenue, displays railroading history with eighty rail cars and locomotives, including Dwight Eisenhower's World War II staff car and the largest steam locomotive in the world. The museum also offers twenty-minute train rides from May to October.

Islam has Mecca; the Catholic Church has St. Peter's Basilica; the spiritual center of Packerdom is Lambeau Field. That every seat here is filled every game, every year, is a testament to the central tenet of the faith: regardless of the number of games won or lost, the Green Bay Packers are the greatest team ever to play the game of football. It was here that Bart Starr, Vince Lombardi, and Ray Nitschke, among others, led the green and gold to victory. At the Green Bay Packer Hall of Fame, across Lombardi Avenue from Lambeau Field, you'll find the past and present of the team from Titletown. Stadium tours begin at the Hall of Fame as well. Lambeau Field and the Packer Hall of Fame are located near the intersection of Oneida Street and Lombardi Avenue-you can't miss the signs from any highway leading into Green Bay.

When you are able to tear yourself away from Lambeau Field (it was hard for me), head out of town on Wisconsin Highway 57 North. Approximately 8 miles out of town, the road reaches the edge of Green Bay (the body of water, that is), right about where Jean Nicolet landed in 1634 as an emissary of New France, to make allies of the locals and establish a relationship for the fur trade. The Winnebago Indians who met him honored the first white man in Wisconsin with a banquet of 120 beavers. At the town of Dyckesville, on the bluff overlooking the beach and the bay, you cross into Door County.

Eleven miles beyond Dyckesville is Brussels, a large Belgian-American settlement. Scattered throughout Door, Brown, and Kewaunee Counties, adjacent to the shores of Green Bay and Lake Michigan, these areas were initially settled in the 1850s. Many of the original structures of the Walloon-speaking Belgians were destroyed in a firestorm that swept across Door County in October, 1871, the same month and year in which the town of

Drive 3: Door County
State Parks and Shoreline

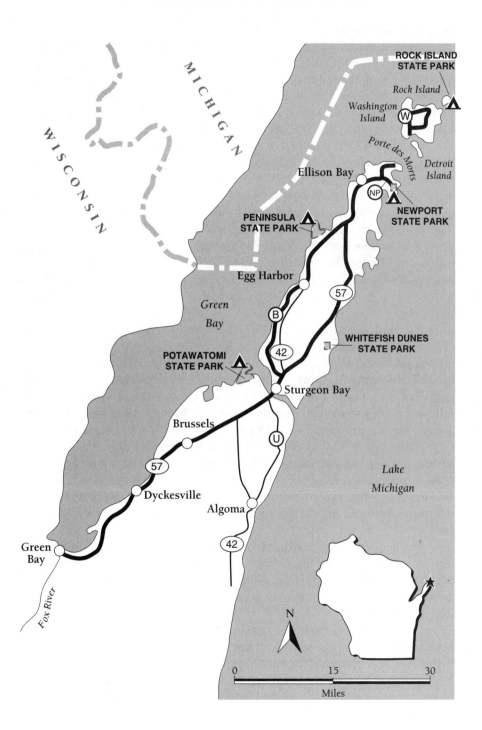

ROCK ISLAND
STATE PARK

Rock Island

*Washington
Island*

W

Porte des Morts

*Detroit
Island*

MICHIGAN

WISCONSIN

Ellison Bay

NP

NEWPORT
STATE PARK

PENINSULA
STATE PARK

Egg Harbor

57

Green
Bay

B

42

WHITEFISH DUNES
STATE PARK

POTAWATOMI
STATE PARK

Sturgeon Bay

Brussels

U

Lake
Michigan

57

Dyckesville

Algoma

42

Green
Bay

Fox River

N

0   15   30
Miles

Peshtigo (Drive 5) and Chicago were destroyed by fire. Red brick houses from the 1880s, as well as many roadside chapels, bespeak Door County's Belgian history today.

Approximately 13 miles farther along WI 57 from Brussels, you'll see a sign for Potawatomi State Park, named for the Native Americans who inhabited Green Bay's shores and islands and called themselves *Bo-de-wad-me*, meaning "Keeper of the Fire." The park is 1,200 acres of upland bordered by steep slopes and rugged limestone cliffs along the shore, with great hiking, biking, and shoreline scenery, as well as 125 campsites.

Back on WI 57, you'll soon cross over Sturgeon Bay (the body of water) and into Sturgeon Bay (the town). Sturgeon Bay (the body of water) originally opened broadly onto Green Bay, but stopped short of (though in sight of) Lake Michigan. Joseph Harris, Sr. led the effort to build the Sturgeon Bay-Lake Michigan Canal, which, when opened to shipping in 1882, connected Green Bay and Lake Michigan at Sturgeon Bay, cut 100 miles of dangerous waters from the Green Bay to Milwaukee and Chicago shipping routes, and fueled the growth of Sturgeon Bay (the town). Shipping and shipbuilding have long been the mainstay of the Sturgeon Bay economy, outlasting the lumbering and limestone quarrying that first brought settlers to the area.

As you leave Sturgeon Bay, you'll notice that WI 57 and Wisconsin Highway 42 are running together. Follow WI 42 when they diverge, just outside of town. Approximately 1 mile outside of Sturgeon Bay, turn left onto Door County Highway BB—follow the scenic drive sign. At the second stop sign on County BB, turn right onto Door County Highway B, and follow this very scenic drive up the coastline, through the woods, and past spendy vacation property. At the intersection with Door County Highway G, County B ends. Follow County G to the left. Immediately after that left turn, you'll see the entrance to a Door County park with a beach, picnic area, fishing pier, and toilets. If you stop here, note that the park road is a one-way, and when you come out of the park you're back on County B. Turn left onto County B, and then left again at the County B/County G intersection.

In the town of Egg Harbor, 4 miles up from the county park, turn left onto WI 42. Outside of Egg Harbor you'll see some of the orchards that produce the fruit for Door County's famous cherry pie. The hilly, forested, farm- and orchard-dotted route continues through the towns of Juddville and Fish Creek.

Peninsula State Park, Wisconsin's largest state park, is located just beyond Fish Creek. Occupying an entire peninsula between the towns of Fish Creek and Ephraim, the park has miles of hiking and biking trails and a whopping 469 campsites. Eagle Bluff Lighthouse, built in 1868, is located in the park along Shore Road, and from early summer to fall, tours of the

A view of Sister Bay in Door County.

lighthouse run from 10 A.M. to 4:30 P.M. Two-hundred-foot Eagle Tower, on the east side of the park, provides spectacular views of the peninsula and Green Bay. The 3,763 acre peninsula has been a summer retreat since the park was created in 1909. In the park's first few years, mothers often spent the entire summer in the park with their children, while their husbands worked in the nearby industries, and paid five dollars for an entire season of camping. The park also housed German prisoners of war near the end of World War II. From 1916 to 1948 two women from St. Louis ran a camp for girls here, and during the Great Depression 208 members of the Civilian Conservation Corps were stationed here and contributed their labor to the development of the park.

As you continue north on WI 42 from the park, you pass through the towns of Ephraim, Sister Bay and Ellison Bay. You are approaching the end of the Door County mainland, with its dense stands of trees and high bluffs overlooking the Bay. Three miles out of Ellison Bay, Door County Highway NP takes you to 2,400-acre Newport State Park, 28 miles of wilderness hiking trails, and 16 backpack-only campsites; fabulous sandy beaches, hidden coves and rocky headlands. The park, once the site of a logging village, was designated a Wilderness Area in 1974 and abounds with wildlife, including deer, foxes, coyotes, porcupines, and raccoons.

Barn on Lake Michigan.

Four miles farther along WI 42, through Gills Rock and over a very winding stretch of asphalt, you hit the bay and the end of WI 42. From here you can take a car ferry across Porte des Mortes ("Death's Door," the straits the Sturgeon Bay-Lake Michigan Canal was built to bypass) to Washington Island. The thirty-minute ferry ride offers beautiful views of the mainland bluffs and the rocky island shores. Washington Island is wooded and quiet, has only one major road (Door County Highway W), and is home to the oldest Icelandic settlement in the United States.

If you're looking to get way out there, leave your car at Jackson Harbor on the northeast side of Washington Island, and take a smaller, passenger-only ferry out to Rock Island State Park. Rock Island was the summer home of inventor C. H. Thordarson (born in Iceland), known for building the first million-volt transformer and later developing equipment for transmitting high-voltage electricity over long distances. While you can take your bicycle to the island, you can't ride it there; the entire island is non-motorized. The wooded, 900-acre island offers a lighthouse, plenty of seclusion, hiking, and camping.

Whether or not you take the ferry out to the islands, head back down WI 42 to Sister Bay and the junction with WI 57. Turn left onto WI 57 as you're going up the hill immediately south of town. As WI 57 cuts across the peninsula you'll see farms and fields, and in some spots the trees form a canopy over the road. At Bailey's Harbor, WI 57 meets the Lake Michigan shore. Seven miles south of Bailey's Harbor is Jacksonport, and approximately 5 miles south of Jacksonport is Door County Highway WD, where a left turn points you toward Whitefish Dunes State Park and the end of this drive.

Whitefish Dunes State Park is home to some of Wisconsin's biggest sand dunes. "Old Baldy," the tallest here, rises 93 feet above the lake shore. Native American artifacts were discovered here in 1985, and excavations of a natural depression near the current Nature Center in 1986 and 1992 unearthed more than 35,000 artifacts, some dating from as early as 100 B.C. The depression was used as a garbage dump by five distinct native cultures nearly continuously for two thousand years. Attracted by abundant fish, game, and chert (a rock similar to flint) for the manufacture of stone tools, as well as the beaches and great scenic canoeing, the North Bay, Heins Creek, Late Woodland, Oneota, and Potawatomi peoples spent their summers here and wintered farther inland. The park has a picnic area, hiking trails, and a swimming beach. Please stay on the trail near the dunes, as they are easily disturbed. If you want to swim, take heed that the shoreline produces strong rip currents in sections; pay attention to the posted warnings.

A left at the park entrance onto WI 57 will take you back to Sturgeon Bay or (for the fanatics) Lambeau Field.

4

Wisconsin Highway 22
Waupaca to Oconto

General description: This drive starts at a convalescent home and ends at a burial mound, but it's fairly lively in between. The route follows Wisconsin Highway 22 from the Wisconsin Veterans Home and Museum on Waupaca's chain of twenty-two spring-fed lakes, to Copper Culture Mound State Park in Oconto on the shore of Green Bay. Oddities found along the way include a town named Embarrass and a piece of the Great Wall of China. WI 22 rolls over hills, through forests, and past lakes and rivers.

Special attractions: Copper Culture Mound State Park, Wisconsin Veterans Home and Museum, the Great Wall of China, The Menominee Logging Museum, Oconto County Forest Machikanee Unit, hiking, fishing, camping, cross-country skiing, wildlife watching.

Location: East-central Wisconsin. The drive starts in King, near Waupaca, and ends at Copper Culture Mounds State Park in Oconto. 85 miles.

Drive route numbers: Wisconsin Highways 22, 55, 47, Waupaca County QQ, Shawano County VV, Oconto County O.

Travel season: Year-round.

Camping: 101 sites at Hartman Creek State Park near Waupaca, 45 sites at Holtwood Park in Oconto, 33 sites at North Bay Shore Recreation Area between Oconto and Peshtigo.

Services: Full services in Waupaca, Shawano, and Oconto, limited elsewhere.

 The drive

This drive begins at the Wisconsin Veterans Museum and Home, in King, 1 mile down Waupaca County QQ from its intersection with Wisconsin Highway 22, east of Waupaca. The 750-bed Wisconsin Veterans Home overlooks Rainbow Lake, the largest lake in Waupaca's twenty-two lake chain of spring-fed lakes. Founded in 1887 by the Grand Army of the Republic for aging and infirm veterans of the Civil War, the home is still used today, and the museum houses war relics and features displays on American war history.

Drive 4: Wisconsin Highway 22
Waupaca to Oconto

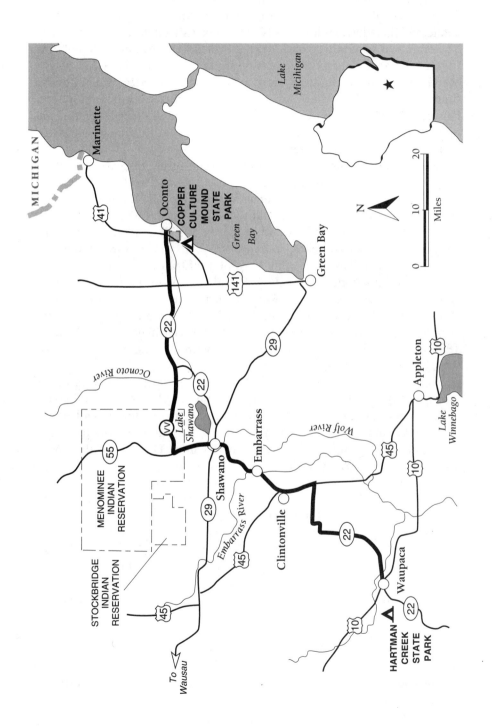

From the museum, turn right on County QQ and then left onto WI 22. At U.S. Highway 10, WI 22 turns right and follows US 10 east for about a mile, and then diverges from US 10 at the next exit and heads into Waupaca. The origins of Waupaca go back to 1849, when five Vermonters hiked from Plymouth, near Sheboygan, to take advantage of lands ceded by the Menominee to the U.S. Government in an October 1848 treaty. They built a flour mill at the falls of the Waupaca River, and built their homes in the area between the Waupaca and Crystal Rivers. By 1852 another flour mill was operating, this one at the nearby falls of the Crystal River, and the settlement had grown large enough to warrant a post office. The Hutchinson House Victorian House and Museum on Main Street displays household furnishings from the 1860s, open Fridays, holidays, and weekend afternoons.

In Waupaca, WI 22 joins forces with Wisconsin Highway 54. Turn right at that intersection. You'll find that dairy farms and corn fields have replaced wheat in the land around Waupaca. WI 22 and WI 54 part company 8 miles out of Waupaca, so follow WI 22 to the left toward Manawa. Named for an Indian brave, this burg of 1,200 on the Little Wolf River attracts cowboys from all over the U.S. and Canada for its annual rodeo in early July. Three miles beyond Manawa, turn right at the intersection with Wisconsin Highway 161 and follow WI 22. A mile later, you'll cross the Wolf River at Symco, a settlement established by German immigrants in the 1880s. Between Symco and the intersection with U.S. Highway 45 there are 9 hilly miles of great views.

At US 45, turn left and follow WI 22/US 45 north through a mixed forest of oak, maple, and white pine to Clintonville. Clintonville boasts Pioneer Park, an eclectic collection featuring the town's first town hall and firehouse, a house made of mortar and firewood, and the town's pet rocks, one of which is a chunk of the Great Wall of China. This may be the closest you ever get to the Great Wall.

Follow WI 22 when it leaves US 45 in Clintonville, and 4 miles down the road you'll come to the town of Embarrass, on the Embarrass River. The river got its name from the nineteenth-century French-Canadian lumberjacks who tried to use it to float logs to the Wolf River at New London. They called it the *Riviere Embarrasser* (*embarrasser* meaning "to impede, obstruct or entangle" in French) after they discovered that its numerous bends, twists, and snags made it useless as a logging river.

Keep on keepin' on, and in 10 miles you're in Shawano (if you want to sound like a local, say it as "Shawn-o"). *Shawano* means "to the south" in both the Ojibwe and Menominee languages, and Lake Shawano marked the southern boundary of Ojibwe tribal territory. In the nineteenth century, a band of Menominee moved here from the Green Bay area in search of good fishing and settled near the lake. The city of Shawano is built in and around this settlement.

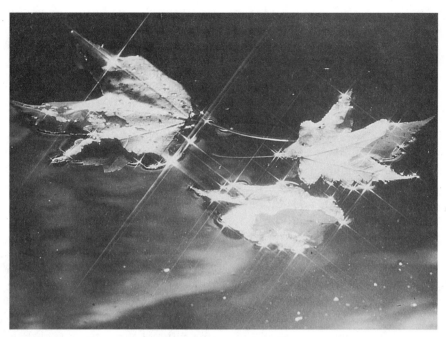

Autumn leaves on a glittering lake. WISCONSIN DEPARTMENT OF TOURISM PHOTO

WI 22 joins Wisconsin Highway 29 in Shawano, and then both roads intersect with Wisconsin Highway 55. Turn left on WI 55 and travel to the Menominee Indian Reservation, 5 miles north of Shawano (notice how much Lake Shawano frontage the Menominee got out of that deal). Highway 55 here was a part of a military road that ran from Green Bay to Lake Superior and was used extensively by loggers and lumbermen as a supply route after the Civil War.

Keshena, 2 miles beyond the reservation border, is home to the Menominee Logging Museum, owned by the Menominee tribe. The museum bills itself as the largest and most complete logging museum in the United States. To get there, go through Keshena, and follow Wisconsin Highway 47 north when it diverges from WI 55. Turn left at Shawano County VV. Open from May to October, seven buildings, including a bunk house, cook shanty, blacksmith shops, camp office, and twenty thousand artifacts evoke the earliest days of Wisconsin's logging industry.

Travel back through Keshena on County VV, and follow it when it turns left and heads out of town. County VV travels east through the southern end of the Menominee Reservation and winds between and around a collection of ten small lakes, the largest of which, Legend Lake, will appear on the left. After 7 miles on County VV you're off the reservation, and you'll find the town of Underhill 5 miles beyond the reservation's border. In Underhill, County VV ends. Take Oconto County U towards Gillett, and after 2 miles turn left, back onto WI 22 east.

Oconto Falls, once a lumber town, is 4 miles further on WI 22. Just south of Oconto Falls is the 8,700-acre Machikanee Unit of the Oconto County Forest. In 1927, when the Wisconsin legislature created the County Forest Crop Law, marketable timber was quickly disappearing. The law provided property-tax incentives for reforestation and today there are more than 42,000 acres in the Oconto County Forest system. The Machikanee Unit offers fishing, hunting, hiking, cross-country skiing, lots of trees and water, and camping, though you need to get a camping permit from the Oconto County Forests and Land office in Oconto. Follow WI 22 when it turns left, just past downtown Oconto Falls, and travel to U.S. Highway 141. To find the forest as a quick side trip, turn right onto US 141 south, and then right again on East Tower Road, approximately 2 miles from WI 22. Otherwise, stick with WI 22.

From US 141 to Copper Culture Mounds State Park in Oconto, the road runs through low, rolling forested hills. You'll see the sign for Copper Culture Mounds State Park when you enter the town of Oconto. Follow the sign and turn right onto Mott Street (it's nearly a hairpin turn), and then head down the left branch of the road at the Y-intersection, and you'll find the park. The Old Copper People lived in northern and eastern Wisconsin approximately 4,500 years ago. Archaeologists named them for their use of copper tools, weapons, and ornaments. The only thing we know about the time they spent in the Oconto area is that they buried their dead in burial mounds here. The copper this group of Copper People used may have come from the Bad River Valley area at Copper Falls State Park (Drive 8), where Copper Culture Indians are known to have extracted the metal. Copper Culture artifacts have also been found at Whitefish Dunes State Park (Drive 3) and Pattison State Park (Drive 10). From the parking lot at Copper Culture Mound, a trail runs along the base of the mounds. Artifacts recovered from an excavation by the Wisconsin Archaeological Survey and the Oconto County Historical Society are housed in the nearby Werrebroek House Museum.

Copper Culture Mounds State Park is the end of this drive. From here, you can check out the Beyer Home Museum and Annex in Oconto (turn left onto Superior Avenue from Main Street/WI 22), which contains pictures and exhibits about the history of early Oconto in a stately Northern Victorian-style mansion. You can also pick up a map to the Oconto Historic District tour of century-old homes built by the local lumber barons.

Holtwood Park in Oconto has forty-five campsites, a picnic area, and showers. Breakwater Park, located at the mouth of the Oconto River, offers great views of Green Bay. U.S. Highway 41 North to Marinette will take you to the Start of Drive 5, and US 41 South to Green Bay will get you to the start of Drive 3.

5

Marinette County
A Tale of Fire and Water

General description: This drive goes through the heart of Marinette County, mostly traveling north along U.S. Highway 141, through lands once denuded of trees and then reforested, and past waterfalls on wooded rivers. The Menominee Indian tribes met the first European fur traders and explorers who came to this part of the state in Marinette County. The recorded history of the county centers around logging, sawmills, fires, railroads, boom towns, bust, and rebirth.

Special attractions: Peshtigo Fire Museum, Amberg State Historical Site, Dave's Falls, Long Slide Falls, hiking, fishing, snowmobiling, canoeing, whitewater rafting, kayaking, camping.

Location: Northeastern Wisconsin. The drive begins in Marinette, north of Green Bay, and ends in Florence at the junction of U.S. Highway 141 and Wisconsin Highway 101.

Drive route numbers: U.S. Highways 41 and 141, Marinette County Highway B, Morgan Park Road.

Travel season: Year-round.

Camping: 32 sites at Morgan Park, 45 sites in Badger Park in Peshtigo, and at the Marinette City Park Campground.

Services: Full services in Marinette, Peshtigo, and Iron Mountain, limited elsewhere.

The drive

This drive begins in Marinette, named in honor of Marinette Farnsworth (baptized Marguerite, though some say her name was Marie Antoinette), a woman of mixed Ojibwe, Menominee, and European heritage who owned a trading post with her husband here in the early nineteenth century. The town, originally the site of a Menominee village, was officially organized in 1855, fourteen years after William Farnsworth (Marinette's husband) received permission from the federal government to build a sawmill and gristmill on Indian land.

The town grew up around two sawmills, Farnsworth's near the mouth

Drive 5: Marinette County
A Tale of Fire and Water

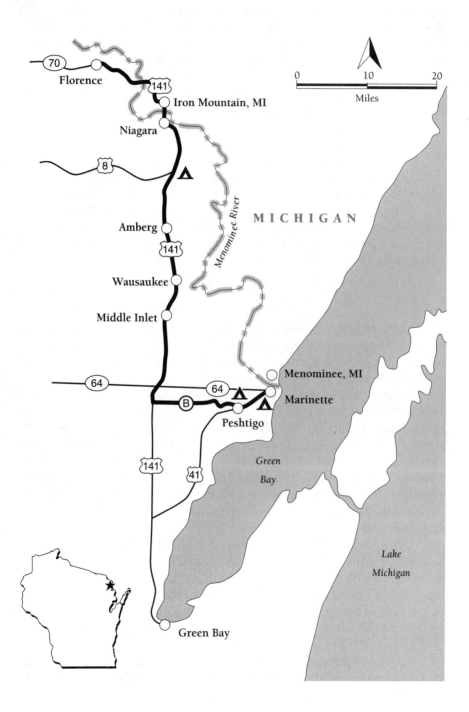

of the Menominee River, and another 2 miles upstream, built in 1856. Ike Stephenson, a long-time area lumberman, eventually gained control of the upstream mill, and used the profits it generated to go into banking, real estate, and the U.S. Senate (1906-1914). Stephenson Island Historical Museum, on Stephenson Island, near downtown, displays artifacts from Menominee Indian culture and the area's logging history.

From Marinette, take U.S. Highway 41 south 7 miles to Peshtigo. In a few short hours on the night of October 8, 1871 (the same night Mrs. O'Leary's cow started the Great Chicago Fire), fire destroyed the village of Peshtigo, leaving it a wasted pile of ashes. The *Peshtigo Times* told the story:

By 10:00 P.M. the roar had thundered to an earth-shaking crescendo and the ferocious winds, now of tornado velocity, ripped through the village in blinding sheets of sand and smoke. The frenzied blaze whipped closer with savage speed, great gusts of wind carried balls of flaming fury hundreds of feet through the air. Like bolts from hell, they burst on the ground and hungry tongues of devouring flame streaked in every direction. In panic for their lives and families, the firefighters flung down their buckets and fled towards their homes— Peshtigo could not be saved.

The spring and summer of 1871 were hot and dry; the creeks dried up and the village wells gave out. By mid-September, the slash piles left by loggers and the dried-out peat bogs were burning almost daily. The evening of October 8, village residents noticed that it was an unusually warm evening for October and that the unnaturally glowing sky to the southwest was considerably bright. A gale force wind had whipped up the embers of the ever-burning smaller fires and driven a wall of flames toward Peshtigo, consuming every building in town but one and leaving eight hundred dead (nearly half the village's population) by morning's light. The Peshtigo Fire Museum and Cemetery is located on Marinette County Highway B and has exhibits on the fire and subsequent Peshtigo history. One block after you cross the Peshtigo River on US 41, follow Oconto Avenue/County B, which angles off to the right, to find them.

Continue out of town on County B. The land here is fairly flat, with alternating farms and forests. After approximately 12 miles, you come to an intersection with U.S. Highway 141 in the town of Coleman. Turn right onto US 141 North and drive approximately 6 miles to a geographical marker just outside of Beaver. From this marker, sitting at a latitude of 45 degrees, 8 minutes, and 45.7 seconds north, it is exactly 3,107.47 miles to the north pole and 3,107.47 miles to the equator.

As you continue north on US 141 towards Middle Inlet and beyond, you are traversing the "cut-over lands" where the agricultural frontier ends.

Dave's Falls on the Pike River.

Corn-belt farmers followed the fall of the forests farther and farther north after World War I, and by 1925 one-third of the county was registered as farm land. What the hopeful farmers didn't know was that the soil would not sustain corn. By 1928, lands suited for forests but not fields fell into tax delinquency and were abandoned. Six of the county's eighteen towns couldn't pay their highway assessments for 1927 because property tax revenue had dropped through the floor.

Six miles north of Middle Inlet, near Wausaukee, there's a great scenic overlook and a historical marker at the top of a hill. From the overlook, you can see the hills and valleys of Marinette County's reforestation program. After the farm failure of the 1920s, most of the county's industry was dedicated to forest products, though only two percent of the county's original marketable timber remained. In 1930, the county registered 14,000 acres as non-taxable forest land and created a county forest in 1933. Today the county has more than a quarter of a million acres in county forests, and the investment has paid off: from 1930 to 1960 the county grossed a total of $1 million from timber sales, and by 1986 timber sales generated $1 million in that year alone.

Continue north 9 miles to the town of Amberg. Just inside the town limits, turn right into a county park and the site of Dave's Falls on the Pike

River. The falls are a short way down the trail leading out from the playground. There's a bridge over the top of the falls and trails along either side of the river. Fifty yards upriver there's another beautiful, though smaller, set of falls. The park also has a picnic area and toilets. Amberg also features a state historical site, a complex which includes the Amberg Museum with great old photos of the area, the town hall, a restored turn-of-the-century home, the original Amberg train depot, and a complete, full-size granite quarry derrick. The complex is 0.3 mile down Marinette County Highway V. It's a right turn from US 141.

Six miles north of Amberg, in the town of Beecher, Marinette County Highway Z heads east (though you need not). Where County Z reaches the Menominee River and the Michigan border, there's a resort in the middle of the river on 82-acre Miscauno Island. The resort, and others like it, was built by the railroad in the early twentieth century in hopes of attracting fare-paying tourists to complement the trade in lumber headed south and settlers headed north. Tourism did not sustain the railroad when the timber ran out, and the rail line to the island was abandoned in 1917. Today the railroad bridge is used for automobiles, and the resort is still in operation.

Continue north on US 141 from Beecher. Approximately 6 miles north of Pembine, Morgan Park Road leads to 50-foot Long Slide Falls on the Pemebonwon River. Turn right onto Morgan Park Road and follow it approximately 2 miles to a right turn. Follow the signs to a parking area; the falls are 0.25 mile down the trail. Smaller Smalley Falls is 0.5 mile along the trail leading upstream from Long Slide Falls. Morgan Park, another 3 miles down Morgan Park Road from the falls, has 32 campsites on Timm's Lake, as well as a swimming beach, boat landing, playground, and great scenery.

Head back to US 141, turn right, and travel to the town of Niagara. The Menominee River has cut a steep-walled gorge here, and the tree-topped bluffs are visible as US 141 rolls through town. Stick with US 141 through Niagara, and you'll cross over the Menominee River and into Michigan. The route turns left where US 141 joins U.S. Highway 2 East, goes through the town of Iron River, and then crosses the Menominee back into Wisconsin. Iron River gets its name from the rich iron deposits found on both sides of the river in the 1870s.

Captain Jefferson Cram, U.S. Army officer, was the first white explorer to document travel through this area when he surveyed the northeast border of the state in 1840 and 1841. The main river channel changes its name upstream of Florence from the Menominee to the Brule River. Cram followed the Brule, which was called *We-sa-co-ta* by the Menominee tribes and forms the border between Wisconsin and Michigan for its 54 miles, back to its source, Lake Brule. He noted the white cedar, pine, poplar, fir, and tamarack along the river, and the rich upland hardwood forests at the top of the river valley. Cram found the area controlled by the Menominee

Whitewater rafting on the Peshtigo River. WISCONSIN DEPARTMENT OF TOURISM PHOTO

tribes, but the Ojibwe often mingled with them.

H. D. Fisher was a sailor before he arrived in the Florence area in 1871 looking for iron. Legend has it that after two years of fruitless searching, he stuck his walking staff with weary frustration into the hillside upon which he was resting and unearthed the hematite he sought. He went on to become quite rich from the proceeds of his mine and is remembered as a philanthropist and civic leader.

The drive ends at the Florence Natural Resource and Wild River Interpretive Center at the junction of US 141 and Wisconsin Highway 101. The center features displays on Indian history, logging and mining history, and local natural history. You are now at the far eastern edge of Wisconsin's great northern forests. Drives 6 and 7 are closest to you now, and anywhere you go from here is guaranteed to be scenic.

6

Lakewood Auto Tour
Nicolet National Forest

General description: This drive follows the 65-mile Lakewood Auto Tour developed and maintained by the Nicolet National Forest. The roughly circular route explores the forest and forest industries past and present at seventeen tour stops.

Special attractions: Cathedral Pines great blue heron rookery, Mountain Fire Tower, logging camp ruins, hiking, fishing, camping, wildlife viewing, canoeing.

Location: Northeastern Wisconsin. The drive starts and ends at the Lakewood Ranger Station in Lakewood, on Wisconsin Highway 32.

Drive route numbers: Wisconsin Highways 32 and 64, Oconto County Highways F, T and W, Forest Roads 2121, 2122, 2283, 2336, 2283, 2118, 2106, 2319, 2102, 3877, 2101, Fanny Lake Road, Grindle Lake Lane.

Travel season: Year-round.

Camping: 34 sites at Boot Lake, 30 sites at Bagley Rapids, as well as no-fee, no-service sites near tour stops 2, 8, and 17.

Services: Limited services in Lakewood and Mountain.

 The drive

This drive highlights one of the ironies of our modern life: managed nature. The Forest Service, not surprisingly a branch of the U.S. Department of Agriculture, plants trees and cultivates the plantations for maximum forest product (pulpwood for paper as well as lumber) harvest. Trout streams are stocked from local fish hatcheries. Wildlife habitat is manipulated to promote popular game species such as grouse, ducks, and white-tailed deer.

Yet this beautiful forest is about as close as we can get to "nature." The original forests were wiped away by loggers and replaced by plantations and carefully parcelled hunting grounds. The trees are here primarily because not much else will profitably grow here; this is the forest's salvation, and its future. With that in mind, head for the Lakewood Ranger Station.

Drive 6: Lakewood Auto Tour
Nicolet National Forest

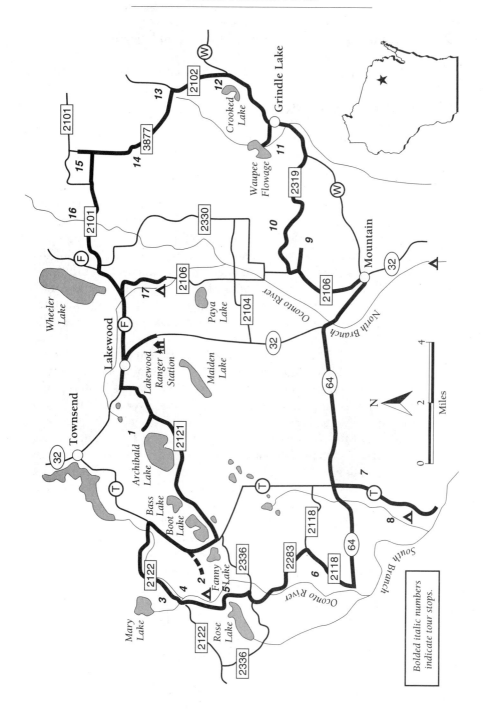

Bolded italic numbers indicate tour stops.

As you may have guessed from the route numbers listed, this drive takes you bombing through the backwoods. Logging trucks are not uncommon on these roads. The route is erratically paved, and a few of the potholes may make you wince, so you've been warned.

This route starts at the Lakewood Ranger Station on Wisconsin Highway 32, where you can get all kinds of information on recreational opportunities in the forest. Head north from the ranger station on WI 32 for 1.5 miles, look for the Auto Tour sign, and turn left onto Forest Road (FR) 2121/Archibald Lake Road. You're headed for tour stop number 1, Cathedral Pines. Incidently, there's a wayside with a scenic overlook and picnic area about 200 yards north of the WI 32 and FR 2121 intersection. The drive goes in a circle, so it's a good place to stop at either end of the drive.

Follow FR 2121 for 1.5 miles, take a right at the Auto Tour sign onto an unmarked gravel road, and travel about 0.5 mile to Cathedral Pines. The white pines and eastern hemlocks here escaped the logging fury of the early 1900s and stand as an example of the forest that once was. Many of the white pines here shelter the approximately one hundred nests of a great blue heron rookery; the nesting season is May through July. A hiking trail, leading from the small turn-around at the stop, takes you through the pines and past the rookery. Please respect the herons's space and stay at least 300 feet from the nesting area.

Head back to FR 2121, take a right, and travel about 4 miles to Oconto County T. Watch for the Auto Tour Signs. On the way to the County T intersection, the tour takes a left at a stop sign. At the County T intersection you come to another stop sign. Take a right. Go just over a mile to Fanny Lake Road, and take a left onto the gravel road.

At the end of the road is a trailhead and tour stop 2, the Jones Spring Area. Fanny Lake is 0.25 mile down the trail. Ten miles of hiking and cross-country skiing trails around the lake will take you to five walk-in campsites. The 2,000 acre Jones Spring Area is managed for non-motorized recreation and is a great spot for wildlife watching.

Drive back to County T and turn left. Go 1.5 miles to FR 2122/Sawyer Lake Road, and keep a sharp eye on the Auto Tour signs, as they'll help you through the next couple of intersections. The route takes a left, then a right at a stop sign, and then an immediate left (all the while on FR 2122) as it leads to tour stop 3, 2.9 miles from the intersection of FR 2122 and County T. A short walk down the trail here takes you to a wildlife opening, constructed to create habitat for a variety of species including ruffed grouse, butterflies, songbirds, and white-tailed deer.

Continue on FR 2122 a third of a mile to a parking area and tour stop 4, the Jones Spring Impoundment. Down the trail a short way is a dam on Mary Creek. Look over the impoundment and you'll see boxes built for wood ducks to nest in. Few of the local trees are big enough to provide the

Logging camp ruins.

cavities wood ducks use for their nests.

Go back to FR 2122, take a left, and go to FR 2283/Setting Lake Road. Follow FR 2283 for 2 miles to tour stop 5, wetlands. Once considered useless swamps that were best filled, wetlands are now recognized as an important part of the ecosystem, filtering silt and chemicals out of flowing water and providing flood control and wildlife habitat. Wetlands once covered twenty-five percent of the state.

Continue 0.8 mile on FR 2283 to FR 2336/Rose Lake Road and take a right—it's almost a U-turn. Go 0.3 mile to FR 2283/Sauls Lake Road and take a left, and then travel 2.5 miles to FR 2118. Turn right. A half mile down FR 2118 is tour stop 6, the Oconto River Seed Orchard. Founded in 1967, the orchard provides seedlings for the Lake States National Forests. From the road you can see the immense white pines which produce some of the seeds for the orchard. The orchard office is open to visitors on Wednesdays from 2 to 4 in the afternoon, and orchard staff can answer questions and give tours at that time. The office is 0.8 mile farther along FR 2118. Go through the gated entrance and bear left at the first intersection.

Follow FR 2118 for another 0.7 mile to the stop sign at the intersection with Wisconsin Highway 64. Turn left and travel 3.5 miles to County T. Turn right and drive 0.9 mile to tour stop 7, a stand of red pines that started from natural seeding before the turn of the century. Most of the red pines in the Nicolet were planted after 1930. The stand has been thinned over the years for pulpwood and lumber, and to allow the remaining trees optimum conditions for profitable growth. Many of these trees will be harvested around the year 2000 for lumber.

Continue south on County T for 0.5 mile to tour stop 8, site of the Bear Trail Fire. In 1961, an angler's errant match ignited a blaze which traveled 0.75 of a mile in 20 minutes, jumped across the road you're on and claimed a total of 550 acres. The fire was named for the bears that were once abundant here. Turn around and head back to WI 64, or if you're ready to camp, there are two great campsites less than a mile farther along County T. There is no fee to camp at these sites.

Turn right on WI 64 and follow it east approximately 5 miles to WI 32. Turn right onto WI 32 and go approximately 3 miles to FR 2106/Oconto County W. Turn right, then left immediately to follow FR 2106. After about 2 miles, you'll come to tour stop 9. It's on the right near the bottom of a hill. You can either drive up the short but very rough gravel road (my car sounded like a pinball machine going up this road), or (if, unlike me, you care about your wheel alignment) walk up to the Mountain Fire Tower. The tower was constructed in 1934, one of twenty fire-spotting towers built in the Nicolet during the 1930s. Most of the towers were dismantled when airplanes took over fire-spotting duties, but the Mountain Fire Tower has survived as a relay station for the Oconto County Sheriff's Office. Climb to the top if you dare.

Continue north on FR 2106 for 0.2 mile and take a right at the Auto Tour sign onto FR 2319/Sunrise Lake Road. Among the maples, basswood, birch, and aspen you'll see large boulders strewn about. These are glacial erratics, rocks picked up and brought here from as far away as Canada by the glaciers fifteen thousand years ago. The rocks were trapped in the glacial ice and carried great distances, only to be left where they lay when the glacier melted.

After 3.2 miles on FR 2319 you'll find tour stop 10 on the right side of the road. In 1979, aspen on the north side of the road were harvested for pulpwood and to allow the pines room to grow. As the pines grow larger, they will consume most of the sunlight and choke out the aspen. The area on the south side of the road was clearcut in 1989, and subsequently claimed by the opportunistic aspen. Sometime between 2029 and 2039, these aspen will mature and be harvested for paper.

Continue 1.5 bumpy miles to County W and take a left at the stop sign. Follow County W 1.8 miles into the town of Grindle Lake. Fifty yards after you cross the town limits, take a left onto Grindle Lake Road. Follow the dirt road and the sign to Waupee Dam, tour stop 11. The Waupee Dam bottles up one of the countless trickles of water in the area, creating wetland habitat for waterfowl. The forest service built an osprey platform here in 1989, and bald eagles nest and fish here as well.

Go back to County W, take a left, and continue north 1.7 miles to FR 2102/LaFave Road. Take a left onto FR 2102 and go 0.1 mile to tour stop 12, a pine plantation. The plantation will be thinned when these trees are about thirty years old, again at forty years, and the remaining trees will be harvested later. Hardwoods will likely grow underneath the thick canopy and succeed the pines.

Continue on FR 2102 about 2 miles and turn left onto FR 3877/Holts Ranch Road. Half a mile down FR 3877 you find tour stop 13. In 1984, 115 acres of jack pine were clearcut here in an attempt to stop the spread of both a tree disease and an insect infestation. This area has been replanted with red pine.

Go another 2 miles on FR 3877 to tour stop 14, the site of a logging camp used from the late 1800s to the early 1900s, and then abandoned. The four low, stone walls of the camp cookhouse are all that is left. You can still walk on the building's foundation, an outcropping of granite laid bare by the scraping of the glacier.

Stick with FR 3877 another 1.5 miles to tour stop 15, Forbes Spring, headwaters of Forbes Creek, a cold-water trout stream and a tributary of the Thunder River. Its trout are stocked from the nearby Thunder River Fish Hatchery. Park next to the Auto Tour sign pointing straight into the woods and head about 200 yards down the wet and spongy trail on the left side of the road to the spring. The boardwalk at the end of the trail takes you right out into the pond surrounding the spring.

Turn around and head back down FR 3877 0.25 mile to FR 2101/Smyth Road and turn right. After 1.3 miles you come to a bridge over the Oconto River, tour stop 16. From here to Chute Pond, 3 miles south of the town of Mountain, the river runs fast over rapids, great for canoeing and trout fishing.

Follow FR 2101 2.8 miles to County F and turn left. Go 0.7 mile to FR 2106/Old 32 and turn left again. In a moment you come to McCaslin Brook Ruffed Grouse and Woodcock Management Area, the 17th and final stop on the tour. This area is specifically managed to support ruffed grouse and woodcock by actively encouraging the aspen these game birds prefer for food and shelter. About 0.3 mile farther down the road there's a great campsite next to a small brook. There is no charge to use this site. If you cross a bridge before you find the site, you've gone too far. To finish off this drive, head back down FR 2106 to County F, take a left, and go 2 miles to WI 32 in Lakewood, where you started.

7

Northern Highland
American Legion State Forest
Lake Country

General description: This 105-mile drive runs through the Northern Highland American Legion State Forest and the Lac du Flambeau Indian Reservation. The area has one of the highest concentrations of lakes in the world. The gravel, sand, and clay left behind by the glacier in its final retreat ten thousand years ago support an abundance of both pines and hardwoods. The lakes brim with trophy fish, the woods abound with wildlife, and all manner of trails criss-cross the forest for year-round northwoods adventures.

Special attractions: Rhinelander Logging Museum, Lac du Flambeau Cultural Center, the world's first modern snowmobile, Snowmobile Racing Hall of Fame, camping, hiking, biking, wildlife watching, fishing, cross-country skiing, canoeing.

Location: North-central Wisconsin. The drive starts in Rhinelander, loops through the forest and ends in St. Germain.

Drive route numbers: Wisconsin Highways 47 and 155, U.S. Highway 51, Vilas County Highways N, K, and W.

Travel season: Year-round.

Camping: 875 sites among 18 state forest campgrounds, Lac du Flambeau Tribal Campground and Marina, various private resorts and campgrounds along the way.

Services: Full services in Rhinelander, limited in Minoqua, Lake du Flambeau, and St. Germain.

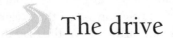 The drive

This drive starts in Rhinelander, home of the Hodag. The myth of this green, horned, spike-tailed, dragon-like critter began in 1896. Local lumberman Gene Shepherd showed his friends a picture of the monster he reportedly pulled from its lair (with the help of a couple of lumberjacks) after putting it to sleep with a chloroform-soaked sponge tied to a pole. Shepherd later admitted that the body was a wood frame covered with ox hides, the

Drive 7: Northern Highland
American Legion State Forest
Lake Country

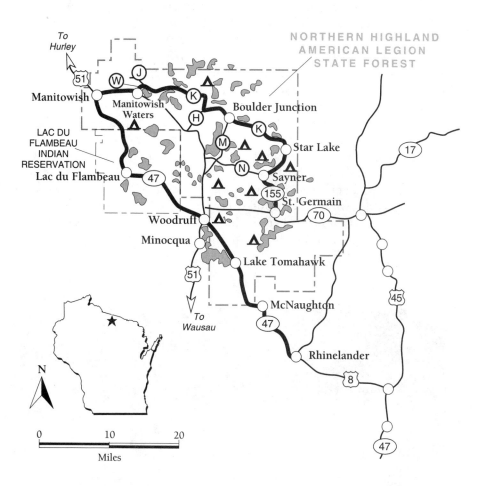

horns and spikes were borrowed from various bulls, and the claws were bent steel rods. The Rhinelander Logging Museum has a replica of the Hodag among its other exhibits on local history. The town was born in 1880 during the logging boom. Originally called Pelican Rapids, the city was renamed for F. W. Rhinelander when he agreed to bring his railroad to town to haul out the area's hardwoods after the pine had all been cut.

At the intersection of U.S. Highway 8 and Wisconsin Highway 47, on the west side of Rhinelander, head north on WI 47 toward McNaughton. Approximately 2 miles beyond McNaughton, WI 47 crosses into the Northern Highland American Legion (NHAL) State Forest. The Northern Highland Geological Province, which includes roughly 15,000 square miles of northern Wisconsin stretching from Rhinelander north to the Michigan border, is the remains of an ancient mountain range once comparable to the Rockies, worn down by erosion over hundreds of millions of years. Established in 1925 to protect the streamflow at the headwaters of the Wisconsin, Flambeau, and Manitowish rivers, the 220,000-acre NHAL State Forest has 18 campgrounds with 875 campsites, as well as 118 canoe campsites and 13 wilderness backpack sites. There are hundreds of miles of logging and town roads, perfect for hiking and biking in solitude. Campers must get a special

Canopied county highway after a rain.

Ballard Lake.

permit from the state forest headquarters for any camping outside of the campgrounds.

Woodruff is 15 miles north of McNaughton on WI 47. The town was planned in 1888 by Alfred Cary, general solicitor for F. W. Rhinelander's Milwaukee, Lake Shore, and Western Railway Company, who bought the land and maintained the timber rights for the railroad. The Dr. Kate Pelham Newcomb Museum, on Second Street, remembers a pioneer physician and exhibits other local historical artifacts.

For a scenic side trip, turn left onto U.S. Highway 51 South and travel 1 mile to Minocqua, known as the island city. The city (it's actually on a peninsula) is surrounded by 2,000-acre Minocqua Lake, as well as several hundred area lakes and ponds. Summer nights in Minocqua bring free waterski shows and the lonely call of the loon. The town is also the northern end of the Bearskin State Trail, which runs along 18 miles of abandoned railroad grade, roughly following US 51.

Continue north on WI 47 from Woodruff. Approximately 3 miles out of town, the road crosses into the Lac du Flambeau Indian Reservation. Created in the same 1854 treaty that created the Bad River Reservation (Drive 10) and the Lac Court Oreilles Reservation (Drive 11), this reservation takes its name from French fur traders who called the place "Lake of the Torches" after seeing the Ojibwe fishing at night from their birchbark canoes by torch-light. Lac du Flambeau has been a permanent Ojibwe settlement since about 1745. The Lac du Flambeau Cultural Center preserves the history and culture of these people and this place, displaying artifacts from the early days of the fur trade with the French, and offers workshops on traditional crafts through the summer. Lac du Flambeau Tribal Campground and Marina offers camping and access to the 10-lake Lac du Flambeau chain.

Roughly 7 miles out of Lac du Flambeau on WI 47, you leave the reservation and re-enter the NHAL State Forest. The land here is swampy and low, a huge expanse of tamarack bogs. In Manitowish, 15 miles out of Lac du Flambeau, turn right onto US 51 South and travel 7 miles to Manitowish Waters. In 1934, Chicago gangster John Dillinger was hiding out and enjoying a summer in the northwoods when the law found him at a Manitowish Waters resort. Two people died in the shootout that followed; Dillinger escaped.

Turn left onto Vilas County Highway W in Manitowish Waters, and then right onto Vilas County Highway K a few miles farther. The canopied County K is a winding track crossing the northern part of the NHAL State Forest passing innumerable lakes. Boulder Junction, approximately 15 miles east of County W, calls itself the "Muskie Capital of the World." Anglers can search out the fabled fish on some of the more than 100 lakes found within 10 miles of town. In Boulder Junction, turn right to follow County K where it joins Vilas County Highway M. Turn left and follow County K where it leaves County M, approximately 2 miles south of Boulder Junction.

The 12-mile stretch of County K, from County M to Star Lake, is also Wisconsin Rustic Road 60. Turn right onto Vilas County N just outside of Star Lake. Travel 8 miles to Sayner, where Carl Eliason built the prototype for the modern snowmobile in 1924. The contraption was a toboggan with a boat-motor-driven single track, and front skis for steering. The Vilas County Historical Museum exhibits Eliason's first, and many subsequent, snowmobiles, as well as Native American artifacts and logging displays. The route turns left in Sayner at the junction with Wisconsin Highway 155, but if you want to see the museum, turn right and go one block. The museum is on the left.

Travel south on WI 155 for 7 miles to St. Germain, the end of this drive. A left onto Wisconsin Highway 70 in St. Germain takes you to the Snowmobile Racing Hall of Fame, featuring historic racing sleds, racing paraphenalia, and histories of Hall of Fame inductees.

You are now deep in the forest. Enjoy!

8

Iron County

Copper Falls State Park to Arrowhead Drive Bridge

General description: The Gogebic Iron Range, stretching from Lake Namekagon (Drive 11) east 80 miles to Bessemer, Michigan is known for two things: iron ore and waterfalls. This 80-mile drive takes you bushwhacking through the Iron Range in search of 10 waterfalls (some of them quite removed from civilization) and Iron County's mining history. There are quite a few unpaved roads on this route and they're not well marked, either, so keep your wits about you.

Special attractions: Copper Falls State Park, Oglebay Norton Mining Company Town, wildlife watching, hiking, fishing, camping, skiing, snowmobiling.

Location: Iron County, northern Wisconsin. The drive begins at Copper Falls State Park, 28 miles south of Ashland and ends at the Arrowhead Drive Bridge over the Turtle River, 3 miles north of Mercer.

Drive route numbers: Wisconsin Highways 169 and 77, U.S. Highways 2 and 51, Vogues Road, Potato River Falls Road, Park Road, Town Park Road, Iron County D and FF, Arrowhead Drive.

Travel season: Year-round. Unpaved roads may be treacherous or impassable in winter.

Camping: Copper Falls State Park, Potato River Falls Town Park, Lake of the Falls County Park.

Services: Full services in Hurley, limited services elsewhere.

 ## The drive

The bushwhacking begins at Copper Falls State Park, which is technically in Ashland County. Don't let this bother you. To get there, take Wisconsin Highway 169 East from Wisconsin Highway 13, just north of the town of Mellon. The park entrance is on the left about 1 mile up WI 169.

Copper Falls State Park boasts three waterfalls on the Bad River, named by French fur traders for the difficulty of its navigation. The Three Bridges Nature Trail, leading from the parking area next to the park office, takes you past all three waterfalls. The landscape is rugged, and the walls of the river gorge reach to 100 feet. The Copper Culture Indians lived here for centuries mining the copper veins. They disappeared about one thousand years ago, leaving behind only a few copper tools and weapons. Around the sixteenth century, the Dakota controlled this area. After the arrival of the French and the beginning of the fur trade, the Ojibwe fought the Dakota for control of the northern forest. Over the course of 150 years, with the help of guns purchased from their French fur trade partners, the Ojibwe eventually drove the Dakota onto the prairies in Minnesota. The Ojibwe continue to live in northern Wisconsin—the route cuts across the southeastern corner of the Bad Lake Reservation just north of the park.

Head back to WI 169 and turn left onto WI 169 East. Approximately 8 miles down WI 169, you cross into Iron County. Turn right onto Vogues Road, 1.2 miles from the county line. You're likely to see a few logging trucks, but the road is in fairly good shape. After following Vogues Road for 3.5 miles, you'll find that the road takes a hairpin left and two other rough-looking roads lead off into the trees; take the hairpin left. After 1.7 miles, take the left fork at the Y intersection (the one with the dead-end sign), and continue another mile. The road terminates when it reaches the river. Park in the clearing on the left side of the road. The falls can be found by hiking about 150 yards up the trail leading out of the parking lot, and then turning

Tying flies at Saxon Falls in Iron County. Wisconsin Department of Tourism photo

Drive 8: Iron County
Copper Falls State Park to Arrowhead Drive Bridge

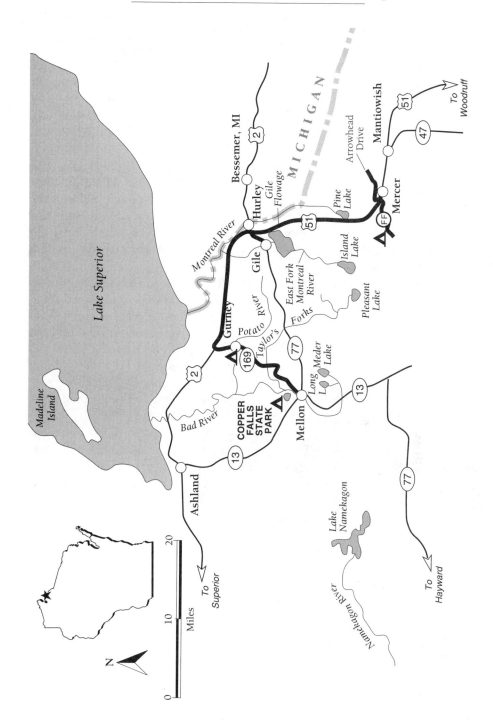

right onto a small footpath. One hundred feet up that path is 25-foot Foster Falls on the Potato River. You may notice some beaver activity in the wide pool below the falls.

Head back the way you came to WI 169 East. Turn right onto WI 169 and travel to Potato River Falls Road in the town of Gurney, the first left just as you enter town. Take this gravel road 1.5 miles to a town park, complete with a couple of campsites with fire rings. Potato River Falls, framed by tall pines, drops 90 feet over the Upper, Middle, and Lower Falls. An easy 100-foot trail leads to an observation deck overlooking the Lower Falls and the deeply-cut river valley. The Upper Falls trail is a little more work, but worth it. Sections are steep and eroded.

Return to WI 169 and turn left. Go 3 miles to U.S. Highway 2 and turn right. This section of US 2 features three great scenic overlooks and two waterfalls. Four and a half miles down the road on the left is the first overlook, and on a clear day you can see Lake Superior, 4 miles away. At the second overlook, another 3.5 miles east on US 2, a historic marker stands above the Gogebic Iron Range.

Continue east on US 2 for 5 miles to Park Road and turn right. Take the next right, Town Park Drive, and travel 0.4 miles to a one-lane bridge. Kimball Park Falls are under the bridge, and there are more scenic rapids a short walk upstream. A picnic area, small playground, and toilets comprise the rest of the park. Head back to US 2 and turn right. Eagle Bluff provides a scenic overlook where you can see for miles over the hilly, wooded iron range. To get up there, turn right onto Iron County D. Where the road crests, take a left into the Eagle Bluff Golf Course and follow the road to the top of the bluff.

Back on US 2, you'll be traveling along the base of Eagle Bluff. Just when you're tempted to look up at the bluff, the two-lane US 2 splits into divided highway. Right where the road splits, there are three bits of pave-ment-your opportunity to take a left across the median and west-bound lane. Find Peterson Falls by crossing at the third one. If you miss it the first time (like I did), take the exit ramp to U.S. Highway 51 South and follow it 0.2 mile to the conveniently located Wisconsin Tourism Information Center. Turn around here, turn left at the exit, and head back the way you came-you'll be going back onto US 2. At the bottom of the US 2 entrance ramp, turn right onto the first gravel road you see. Follow this, even as it turns into a two-rut track into the woods and bends to the right, for 0.2 mile. Where the road stops, park and hike down the trail on the left 0.3 mile to 35-foot Peterson Falls. The cedar, red pine, and maple forest along the river is beautiful even on a rainy day.

The next stops are in Hurley, also known as Sin City. Hurley's Silver Street boasted eighty-seven saloons in 1884, the height of the mining boom. At street level, the buildings on Silver Street were legitimate taverns and

Upper Falls of the Potato Falls, on the Potato River.

merchant shops. Silver Street basements were as often as not converted into private gambling clubs. The second floor of many a Silver Street building was a house of ill repute.

Get back onto US 2 and take the exit for US 51 South into Hurley. At the intersection with Wisconsin Highway 77, turn right onto WI 77 West, and travel approximately 2 miles to Nimikon Street. Turn right at the road 500 feet further. The parking area for Gile Falls is on the left after 100 feet. A short way down the trail leading out of the parking area is an overlook of the 15-foot falls. You can cross over the falls on a snowmobile bridge, upstream from the overlook.

Return to WI 77 and turn left. Just across the bridge over the East Fork of the Montreal River, on the right, a geographical marker memorializes the world's deepest iron mine, a 4,335-foot hole dug over 75 years as the Montreal Mining Company brought 45,747,708 tons of iron ore to the surface. The only planned mining town built in Wisconsin (it has since been abandoned) is farther up WI 77, just a bit on the left. In 1921, the Oglebay Norton Mining Company designed a community with company-owned duplexes and single-family homes which miners could rent for as little as $1.50 per room per year. The historical marker would have us believe that this was an idyllic workers' paradise. Perhaps this is true.

Take WI 77 back to US 51 and turn right for the last stretch of this drive, with two falls on the Turtle River. Travel 21.5 miles through forest and past lakes, and turn right onto Iron County FF. Watch for FF to take a 90 degree turn to the left about three miles down the road. Do not follow it straight here: 5.2 miles from US 2, cross the Turtle River and turn left at the County Park sign. The Turtle River drops 10 feet into Lake of the Falls right next to the parking area. There's a campground and picnic area here as well.

Make your way back, and at the US 51 and County FF intersection, go forward across US 51 onto Arrowhead Drive. Go 0.7 mile to a bridge over 10-foot Rice Lake Falls. The falls could be called a long stretch of rapids when not under high water conditions, which usually occur in spring. That concludes this drive. As you move on to wherever it is you are headed next, keep an eye peeled for the elusive Eastern timber wolf. I was lucky enough to spot one at dusk one evening in this area.

9

Great Divide National Scenic Byway
Into the Woods

General description: Sure, this drive is scenic, being a National Scenic Byway and all. Let's see . . . there's trees and . . . more trees . . .one road . . . 47 miles start to finish . . . crosses the Chequamegon National Forest—the chief feature of which is . . . trees. The first time I drove this route, the batteries in my trusty Radio Shack hand-held tape recorder were low, and when I played the tape back with fresh batteries I sounded like Alvin of "Chipmunks" fame. Then I exposed the film I shot along the way. I hope you have better luck. If you're looking for a vast expanse of forest, you're in the right place. The town of Clam Lake (blink and you're past it) is about the only interruption of the trees on this route. The drive approximately follows a 50-mile section of the "Great Divide," the boundary between the Mississippi Valley watershed and the Great Lakes/St. Lawrence Seaway watershed. At an altitude considerably lower than that of the Continental Divide to the west, this marshy, stream-crossed lowland forest is home to a considerable number of trees and an abundance of wildlife that frolic below the boughs. This, by the way, is a fabulous drive in the fall.
Special attractions: Trees.
Location: The sticks. It's out there. Nordern Wisconsin.
Drive route number: Wisconsin Highway 77.
Travel season: Year-round (trees are non-migratory).
Camping: 15 sites at Moose Lake National Forest Campgound, 66 sites at Day Lake National Forest Campground, 11 sites at East Twin Lake National Forest Campground, plus a few private campgrounds scattered along the way. You also can camp anywhere on National Forest lands as long as the site is at least 50 feet from roads, trails, lakes, and streams.
Services: Good luck.

 The drive

The dynamic French duo of Radisson and Groseilliers were the first European explorers to reach this area and its abundance of furs in 1661. The two traveled along the south shore of the Lake Superior to Chequamegon Bay, north of here, and then made their way inland, using the rivers to reach

Drive 9: Great Divide National Scenic Byway
Into the Woods

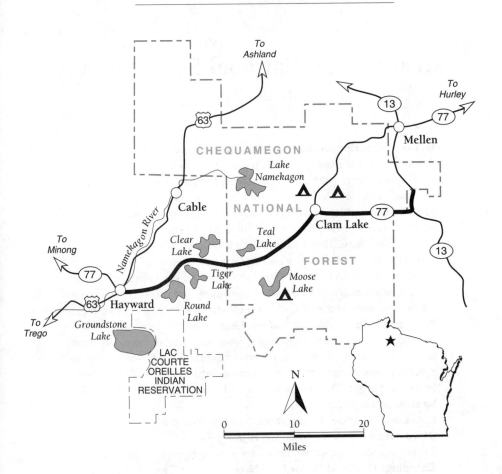

the Ojibwe settlement that is now the Lac Court Oreilles Reservation, located immediately south of Hayward. Radisson and Groseilliers were followed by French *voyageurs*, the grunts of the fur trade, who paddled canoes full of goods and food and equipment up and down the rivers and lakes. The Ojibwe and the French became close allies, and both profited from the fur trade. The British, after kicking French butt in the French and Indian Wars and wresting away the fur trade from France, continued to employ *voyageurs* in the trade. The King of England wanted no more to settle the land than the French had—he only wanted to control fur trade profits. The United States took possession of the land after the War of 1812. The area was deforested in the late nineteenth and early twentieth centuries, farmed briefly, and then reforested to ensure a steady supply of timber, but never settled beyond the infrequent cabins and resorts.

The drive begins in Hayward, at the intersection of U.S. Highway 63 and Wisconsin Highway 77. Head into Hayward on WI 77 East. In late July, the lumberjacks hit town and bring back the flavor of the logging era during the Lumberjack World Championships. The loggers compete in such events as log-rolling and tree-climbing in addition to axe-wielding. Each fall, the town hosts the Chequamegon Fat Tire Festival, touted as the nation's largest off-road bicycling race. In February, skiers throng to Hayward for North America's largest cross-country ski race. Early July features a pow-wow on the Lac Court Oreilles Reservation, when everyone is welcome to take in the dancing, costumes, and games of the Ojibwe tradition. Not nearly last and certainly not least, from mid-April to November, a 143-foot long, 4-story, walk-through fish is the centerpiece of the National Freshwater Fishing Hall of Fame, with 360 antique outboard motors, 400 fish mounts, and antique and historic rods, reels, and accessories on display.

Head out of town and don't slow down for nothin'. Just east of Hayward, you climb up a big hill and drive out of the Namekagon River Valley. Travel 15 miles through lake country and forest to the edge of the

A marshy lake on the Great Divide.

Chequamegon (pronounced *sho-wa-muh-gon*) National Forest, created in 1933. Logging began in this area of the forest in 1825, when a local fur trader got permission from the Ojibwe and Dakota to cut timber in the Chippewa River Valley. Just one hundred years later the trees were gone, and fires raged through the stumps and slash piles of the denuded land. Farmers moved into the clearings left by the loggers, but most of the farms failed. The season was too short and the soil no good for corn or wheat, so after a few meager years the farmers moved on to greener pastures. The Forest Service replanted pineries to provide timber and protect water quality in this area, home to the headwaters of many of northern Wisconsin's rivers—the Namekagon and the Chippewa being chief among those. Today, the forest is managed to provide salable timber, shootable game, and clear water for fishing, in addition to other recreational activities such as camping, hiking, biking, horseback riding, snowmobiling, crosscountry skiing, and canoeing.

The Great Divide here is formed by a line of hills called the Penokee Range. According to the geologists, these hills (and the hills of the Northern Highland (Drive 7) to the east) are what's left of a mountain range that was once as tall as the Rockies. Several million years of intermittent glaciers reduced those mountains to these hills. Rain that falls to the north of the divide flows north into Lake Superior, down the St. Lawrence Seaway, and out into the Atlantic Ocean. Rain that falls to the south of the divide flows south into the Mississippi River and out into the Gulf of Mexico.

Approximately 23 miles out of Hayward, the Lynch Creek Waterfowl Management Area is a great spot for wildlife watching—careful observers are likely to see bald eagles, great blue herons, kingfishers, and a variety of ducks: wood ducks, mallards, hooded mergansers, and ring-necked ducks. You might also spot otters playing in the water or foxes, racoons, coyotes, and deer in the surrounding forest. To find the waterfowl area, turn left onto Forest Road 203 and travel 6.2 miles north to FR 622. Turn left onto FR 622 and drive 0.3 mile to a parking area. The viewing platform, about 0.2 mile down the trail across the road from the parking area, is the best place to observe the birds, otters, and beavers.

About 2 miles past FR 203, you'll see a sign pointing you toward the secluded Moose Lake Campground, which has a beach and boat launch in addition to 15 campsites. To get there, turn right and travel south on FR 174 for 6 miles, then turn right and travel west on FR 1643 for 1.5 miles to the campground.

There are two national forest campgrounds north of Clam Lake. The closest and largest is Day Lake Campground, with 66 drive-in campsites and 3 walk-in campsites, just 1 mile north of Clam Lake on Ashland County Highway GG. At 632 acres, Day Lake has plenty of water for fishing, and legal-size muskies have been caught from the campground's fishing pier.

Highway 77 on the Great Divide.

You can also hike the 0.5 mile Day Lake Interpretive Trail, which wanders along the lakeshore, or have a picnic by the lake at the picnic area. At night, the loons warble into the darkness. The intimate East Twin Lake Campground has 11 campsites on 110-acre East Twin Lake. To get there, travel north on County GG 3 miles beyond Day Lake Campground, turn right onto Forest Road 190, and travel 1 mile to the campground.

Head back to Clam Lake on County GG, turn left onto WI 77, and travel east 14 miles to the intersection with Wisconsin Highway 13. Turn left at the T-intersection to follow WI 77 and travel north 1 mile to the Historical Marker and the end of this drive. The marker begins: "You are now on the Great Divide . . . "

There you have it. More trees than at which you can shake a stick. From here, a short drive 13 miles north on WI 77/WI 13 to Mellen gets you to the start of Drive 8.

10

Lake Superior

Apostle Islands National Lakeshore

General description: For the simple, raw, powerful beauty of nature, perhaps nothing in Wisconsin can match the Apostle Islands found along the shore of Lake Superior north of Ashland. These twenty-two islands, twenty-one of which form the Apostle Islands National Lakeshore, loom tantalizingly close through the Lake Superior mist, inviting travelers to walk through their stands of old growth forests, explore their caves, and gaze back at the towering red cliffs of the mainland coastline. Along this route you'll also see five waterfalls, including the state's largest, and cross both the Red Cliff and Bad River Indian Reservations. Lake Superior weather is fickle, so pack a jacket and a sweater, even in July and August. One day it can be 90 degrees and humid, and the next 50 degrees and raining.

Special attractions: Apostle Islands National Lakeshore, Pattison State Park, Amnicon Falls State Park, Brule River State Forest, Bad River and Red Cliff Indian Reservations.

Location: Northern Wisconsin. The drive starts at Pattison State Park south of Superior and follows the entire length of Wisconsin's Lake Superior shore to a county park in Michigan.

Drive route numbers: Wisconsin Highways 35, 13, and 122, U.S. Highway 2, Bayfield County K, Ashland County H.

Travel season: Year-round. The Madeline Island Ferry runs from the break-up of the lake ice in late March until the eventual freeze-over in late December or early January.

Camping: 59 sites at Pattison State Park, 36 sites at Amnicon Falls State Park, plus many sites in the Apostle Islands National Lakeshore, Brule River State Forest, Chequamegon National Forest and Red Cliff Indian Reservation.

Services: Full services in Superior, Bayfield, and Ashland, limited elsewhere.

 The drive

This drive starts at Pattison State Park, where the Black River drops 165 feet over Big Manitou Falls, Wisconsin's highest waterfall. The Ojibwe Indians who lived here at the time of the arrival of Europeans called the falls

Gitchie Monido, and believed they could hear the voice of the Great Spirit in the tumbling waters. Listen carefully. The Old Copper Culture Indians were here as well, turning the copper they found in and near the park into tools and weapons 4,500 years ago. You'll find the park 9 miles south of Superior on Wisconsin Highway 35. The park entrance will be on your left, but to get to the falls, go past the entrance and up the hill. Turn right onto Douglas County B and park in the lot. You can view the falls from a scenic overlook a short way down the trail across the road. Upstream from the overlook a bridge crosses the top of the falls, and you can see the falls from a different angle from the other side of the river. For the more adventurous, a trail leads downstream from the overlook, descending 200 feet into the Black River valley for half a mile, and then dead-ends; the hike back up is not for the faint of heart. The park entrance back on WI 35 leads to a fifty-nine-site campground, picnic area, and swimming beach.

From the park, take WI 35 north to Superior. In the middle of downtown Superior, at the intersection with Belknap Street and U.S. Highway 2, turn right and follow US 2 1.5 miles to Lake Superior. US 2 turns right when it reaches the lake, and Barkers Island is immediately to your left. From the intersection you'll see the S.S. *Meteor,* the world's only remaining whaleback freighter, built in 1886 and now a maritime museum offering daily tours from May to September. On the right side of US 2, 4 blocks down from the *Meteor,* is the Fairlawn Museum and Mansion. The forty-two-room mansion was once the residence of Superior's second mayor, lumber baron and Pattison Park namesake Martin Pattison. The museum exhibits feature local, merchant marine, and Native American History.

Continue east on US 2 through town, and on your left you'll see the largest coal and iron docks and grain elevators in the world. Lake Superior is the largest body of fresh water in the world (and with an average temperature of 39 degrees Fahrenheit it ranks among the coldest), covering 31,820 square miles at 600 feet above sea level, with a depth up to 1,302 feet. For a good view of Superior Harbor, the western terminus of the St. Lawrence Seaway System, turn left onto Moccasin Mike Road just after US 2 becomes a divided highway on the eastern edge of town. A left onto Wisconsin Point Road 2.5 miles from Moccasin Mike Road takes you 4 miles out onto Wisconsin Point, the harbor's natural breakwater, with wildlife viewing, beach combing, picnicking, and (brrr!) swimming.

Approximately 2 miles out of Superior on US 2, take the Wisconsin Highway 13 exit and cross over US 2 (follow the signs to Apostle Islands National Lakeshore and Bayfield). A right onto Douglas County U, 3 miles from US 2, takes you to Amnicon Falls State Park. The Amnicon River splits into two branches, which plunge over three 30-foot waterfalls here. A hiking trail leading from the south parking lot takes you onto the large island in the middle of the river from which you can view all three falls. The park

Drive 10: Lake Superior
Apostle Islands National Lakeshore

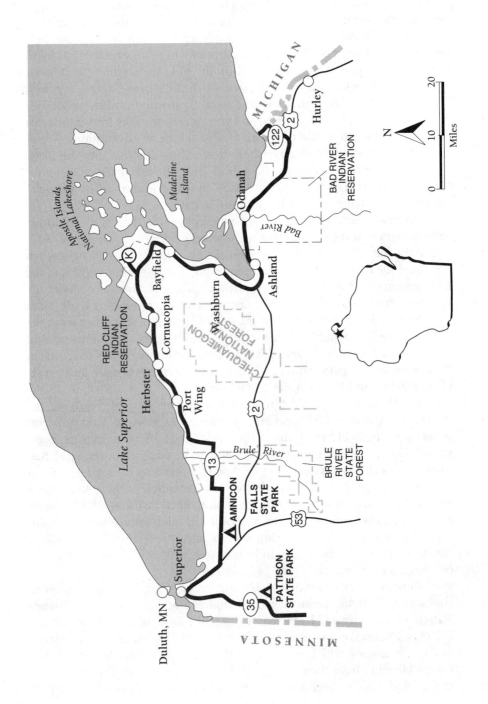

also has thirty-six campsites, a playground and a nature trail.

Continue east on WI 13. The land here is flat and swampy, except where it's deeply cut by the many rivers and streams. After a sharp left turn followed by a sharp right turn, WI 13 enters the Brule River State Forest and descends into the Brule River valley. The red-pine-lined Brule has no waterfalls, but its numerous long stretches of class III-IV rapids make it a fabulous kayaking and whitewater canoeing river. You can rent equipment for such adventures from outfitters in Brule, a few miles south on Douglas County H. WI 13 takes another sharp left at the intersection with County H on the other side of the Brule valley. Stay with WI 13 as it runs north through the forest, near the mouth of the Brule, and then takes a sharp right to roll along the lakeshore.

On the left side of the road, after you cross into Bayfield County and over Fish Creek, is a turnout where you can stop and admire the lake. For 25 forested miles, WI 13 follows the shoreline and runs through the towns of Port Wing, Herbster, and Cornucopia. The forest here is mostly hardwood, with some stands of pine as well. The beach on the east side of the bay at Cornucopia was once a popular Indian camping ground. According to an old legend recorded on a historical marker near here, one spring a few lodges of Ojibwe from La Pointe encamped here. When the chief returned from hunting one day, he found that a large party of Foxes had murdered all but two of his people. He traveled to the Foxes's village, and, finding them about to torture his young son, traded his own life for his son's. The son returned to relatives at La Pointe, and his story brought quick revenge.

Outside of Cornucopia WI 13 leaves the lake. The 12 miles of mainland shoreline east of Cornucopia are the mainland part of the Apostle Islands National Lakeshore. Approximately 10 miles out of Cornucopia, turn left onto Bayfield County K, and then left again approximately 2.5 miles later to Little Sand Bay and a National Lakeshore Visitor Center. President Richard Nixon signed the legislation establishing the Apostle Islands unit of the National Park System in 1970. The Little Sand Bay Visitors Center has information on cruises through the islands and camping, as well as interpretive displays on human and natural history, hiking on the beach, and views of Sand and York islands.

Head back down the road from the visitors center and turn left at County K. You're now traveling through the Red Cliff Reservation, home to the Red Cliff band of Ojibwe. Where County K meets WI 13, turn left. The town of Red Cliff is the hub of the reservation, with full services (including a casino). The reservation has great hiking along the forested red cliffs from which it takes its name, as well as a marina and campground.

Apostle Island National Lakeshore Headquarters is found in an imposing brownstone building (once the county courthouse) in Bayfield. Built on a hill overlooking the lake and Madeline Island, Bayfield has a number of

Big Manitou Falls in Pattison State Park is Wisconsin's highest waterfall—165 feet.

large Victorian homes lately pressed into service as bed and breakfasts. In Bayfield you'll find sailing and scuba diving tours, fishing charters, sea kayak adventures, and more trinket shops than you can shake a stick at.

From Bayfield you can take a car ferry across to La Pointe on Madeline Island. Ojibwe tradition holds that the island was a gathering place and refuge for the tribe, who were pushed westward from their homeland in the St. Lawrence River Valley by another group of Native Americans about the time of Columbus's arrival in the New World. They called the place *Moningwunakauning*, "Place of the golden-breasted woodpecker." They built a large village and lived here for more than one hundred years. Then evil days came—stories are told of corrupt leadership and organized cannibalism, possibly the result of a famine. The tribe rose against its leaders and the people left the island, scattering in small bands across the lands around Lake Superior. The Ojibwe may have already been armed with French guns obtained from French adventurers who traveled deep into the wilderness and traded with the natives without official knowledge or permission. As the bands sought lands away from *Moningwunakauning*, they used their guns against the Dakota and the Foxes, eventually pushing both groups from the northwoods around the big lake. The memory of the events that drove the Ojibwe from the island were strong enough to keep any Ojibwe from returning, and the first whites to leave a record of their visit to the island in 1659 found Huron and Ottawa bands, but no Ojibwe.

Madeline Island is the only one of the twenty-two Apostle Islands that is not a part of the National Lakeshore. The French built their first fort here in 1693 to protect the trade in furs, and Madeline Island was the center of the Lake Superior trade for France until the fall of New France to the English in 1763. The Madeline Island Historical Museum, just a block from the ferry landing at La Pointe, presents three hundred years of the island's history. For a quick tour of the island, head out of La Pointe on Middle Road/Ashland County H. At the intersection with Black's Shanty Road, go forward to get to the 9 miles of hiking trails, caves, lagoon, and sixty campsites at Big Bay State Park, or turn left and follow County H to continue the tour. Turn right at Big Bay Road/County H, and then left onto North Shore Drive where County H ends. The drive along the north side of the island offers great views of Stockton, Michigan, Hermit, and Basswood Islands.

Back in Bayfield, continue on WI 13 south for 20 miles to the intersection with US 2. You'll pass through Washburn on the way, home of the Chequamegon National Forest Washburn Ranger Station, where you can find lots of information on recreation and camping in the National Forest just east and south of here. Turn left onto US 2 from WI 13 and travel to Ashland.

Ashland first prospered in the 1870s when the completion of the Wisconsin Central Railroad brought settlers and money to the area. During the iron mining boom (late 1880s to the turn of the century) Ashland grew again as an important maritime and rail transport center for iron ore from the Gogebic Iron Range (Drive 8). The Ashland Historical Society Museum, in a Classical Revival-style mansion, offers Victorian room displays and Ashland history.

Follow US 2 10 miles out of Ashland to Odanah (*odanah* in Ojibwe means "village"), the largest town on the Bad River Indian Reservation. The French named the river here *Mauvaise* ("Bad"), because it was such a hassle to navigate. The Ojibwe call it the *Mushkeezeebi* ("Marsh") River. This reservation, along with others at Lac du Flambeau (Drive 7) and Lac Court Oreilles south of Hayward (Drives 7 and 9), was created in an 1854 treaty with the U.S. government. The treaty was something of a victory for the Ojibwe, as the U.S. government initially wanted to move all Lake Superior Ojibwe to the plains west of the Mississippi.

Travel 16 miles on US 2 East to Wisconsin Highway 122, the last leg of this drive. Just before WI 122 on US 2 there's a scenic overlook on the left side of the road; on a clear day you can see the lake glittering 4 miles away. Turn left onto WI 122 North, travel 4 miles to the Montreal River and the Michigan border, cross both, and turn left onto a gravel road exactly 0.5 mile from the bridge. A trail leads from the parking lot and then splits into two trails. The upper trail is short and leads to a panoramic view of the lake from the top of the high cliffs. The lower trail leads to the bottom of the Montreal River valley and then back upstream along the river. To find 90-foot Superior Falls, follow the faint trail past and behind the hydroelectric facility (note the warnings about unexpected high water), and keep following the river bank until you catch a glimpse of the falls.

From here you can camp at the Iron County Park you passed (turn right on Iron County A from WI 122) or head to Copper Falls State Park and the start of Drive 9.

11

Namekagon River

St. Croix National Scenic Riverway

General description: This 85-mile drive follows the Namekagon River, one of the two branches of the St. Croix National Scenic Riverway, as it winds its way through northwestern Wisconsin. There are few towns but many resorts along this wooded, lake country drive, and you're as likely to see beavers, deer, and other wildlife as you are people.

Special attractions: St. Croix National Scenic Riverway, Chequamegon National Forest, National Freshwater Fishing Hall of Fame, camping, fishing, hiking, biking, wildlife watching, cross-country skiing.

Location: Northwestern Wisconsin. The drive starts north of Danbury and ends east of Cable.

Drive route numbers: Wisconsin Highway 77, Washburn County Highways E, F, and K, U.S. Highway 63, Bayfield County Highways M and D.

Travel season: Year-round.

Camping: Lake Namekagon Federal Campground, many private resorts and campgrounds along the way.

Services: Full services in Hayward, limited elsewhere.

 The drive

This drive starts at the intersection of Wisconsin Highways 35 and 77, 2 miles north of Danbury. Take WI 77 east. For the first 30 miles of this drive, you won't run across any towns, but there are still people. The Lower Namekagon is prime resort country, where trees, lakes, and campgrounds abound. The entire 98 miles of the Namekagon's length is protected as the St. Croix National Scenic Riverway, created in 1968. The sandy soil here is perfect for pines.

All along this route, you'll see signs for canoe landings—so many, in fact, that you may feel you've chosen the wrong mode of transport. Any one of the landings is a great place to stop for a picnic lunch, a stroll, or a wade in the chilly river. Some landings are as far as 4 miles from the main route, but none of them is difficult to find. If the compulsion overpowers you to find out what canoeing frenzy is all about, you can't do much better than

Drive 11: Namekagon River

St. Croix National Scenic Riverway

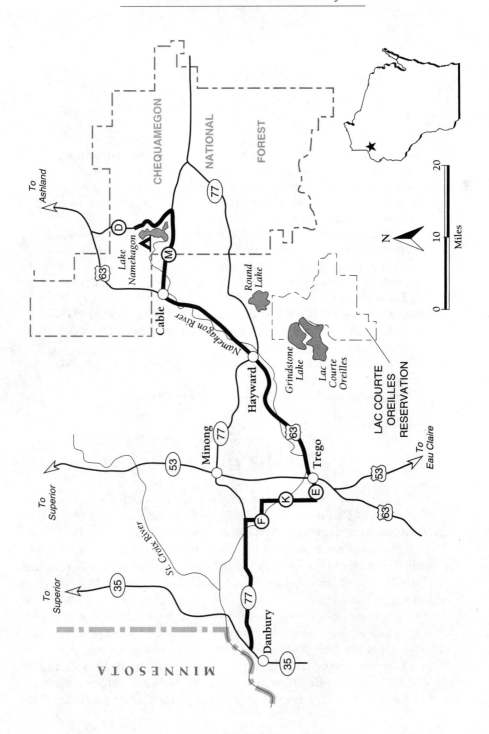

the Lower Namekagon for a lazy float down a river. There are few rocks and no real rapids, and other than the regularly-spaced, canoe-only campsites, only the highway bridges remind you of the surrounding civilization.

Just after you cross into Washburn County, there's a scenic overlook that will give you your first view of the winding Namekagon. Approximately 5 miles from the Washburn county line, turn right onto Washburn County F to follow the river where it turns south. Slow down considerably for this hairpin turn. You'll notice red and jack pines, wetlands, lakes, and tamarack bogs. Turn right where Washburn County K joins County F, and where they separate 2 miles later, follow County K. If you look upstream at the bridge where County K crosses the river, you'll notice some whitewater. These are harmless but fun-to-ride standing waves, created by the high volume of water being squeezed into a small channel, not submerged rocks-this is about as rough as the Namekagon gets. Approximately 4 miles beyond the bridge, turn left at the intersection onto Washburn County E.

When you get to Trego approximately 3 miles later, turn left onto U.S. Highway 53/U.S. Highway 63, and then bear right, following US 63, where the highways diverge. On the eastern edge of Trego is the Trego St. Croix National Scenic Riverway Visitor Center, with interpretive displays on trap-

Beaver house on a small lake.

The unmistakable profile of the National Freshwater Fishing Hall of Fame in Hayward. WISCONSIN DEPARTMENT OF TOURISM PHOTO

ping, logging, natural history, and Native American history, plus information on canoeing the Namekagon, and hiking and camping in the area. US 63 hugs the winding river for the next 40 miles.

You'll pass through the towns of Earl and Spring Brook as you roll through a mixed forest of hardwoods and conifers on your way to Hayward, 21 miles from Trego. Hayward is a year-round northwoods mecca. Each fall, the town hosts the Chequamegon Fat Tire Festival, touted as the nation's largest off-road bicycling race. In February, huge numbers of skiers throng to Hayward for North America's largest cross-country ski race. In late July, the lumberjacks hit town for the Lumberjack World Championships, which includes such events as log-rolling and tree-climbing in addition to axe-wielding. Early July features a pow-wow on the nearby Lac Court Oreilles Reservation. Not last and certainly not least, from mid-April to November, a 143-foot long, 4-story, walk-through fish is the centerpiece of the National Freshwater Fishing Hall of Fame, with 360 antique outboard motors, 400 fish mounts, and antique and historic rods, reels, and accessories. It is, quite honestly, a fisherman's fantasy fishing museum.

Continue north on US 63 for 17 miles to Cable. You'll pass beaver houses, cranberry bogs, and the ubiquitous canoe landings. Turn right on Bayfield County M in Cable. Two blocks from US 63, the Cable Natural History Museum appears on your left. The museum features regularly-changing wildlife exhibits including birds of prey, songbirds, mammals, and insects. Annexed to the museum is the Forest Lodge Library, a log structure built as a community library in 1925 with a massive stone fireplace and hardwood floors. Both are open year-round.

Approximately 5 miles out of Cable you cross into the Chequamegon National Forest, with innumerable recreational opportunities in its several wilderness areas, including hiking, biking, camping, fishing, canoeing, cross-country skiing, and snowmobiling. Backcountry camping is permitted throughout the forest as long as the site is at least 30 feet from any trail or water's edge. Turn left on Bayfield County D, 5 miles from the forest border (don't be fooled by a road called Old D—that's not the one you want). County D follows part of the eastern shoreline of Lake Namekagon, the tenth largest natural lake in the state and the headwaters of the Namekagon River. There is a significant amount of resort development along the lakeshore, but even the resorts can't detract from the lake's beauty.

Approximately 5 miles down County D from County M is a 31-site Lake Namekagon National Forest Campground and the end of this drive. Turn left at the sign, and then left again into the campground. The picnic area on the lake at the end of the road is a beautiful and quiet spot to watch the sun set over the lake.

12

St. Croix River
Prescott to Riverside

General description: The St. Croix River has two faces—the lower and the upper. The lower St. Croix (from Prescott to St. Croix Falls) is dotted with river towns that began as ferry points and lumber mills. On rolling hills between the towns, farms are interspersed with stands of trees. The upper St. Croix, one of the eight original riverways protected by the National Wild and Scenic Rivers Act of 1968, is a place of forests and State Wildlife Areas that support a great variety of woodland creatures, including the recently returned Eastern timber wolf. This drive follows the St. Croix River for 130 miles where it forms the border between Wisconsin and Minnesota.

Special attractions: Kinnickinnic State Park, Interstate State Park, Gandy Dancer State Trail, Fish Lake State Wildlife Area, Crex Meadows State Wildlife Area, Governor Knowles State Forest, hiking, mountain biking, rock climbing, canoeing, fishing, cross-country skiing.

Location: Wisconsin's western border. The drive begins in Prescott and ends just south of Riverside.

Drive route numbers: Wisconsin Highway 35, Pierce County Highway F, Interstate Highway 94, WI 87, Burnett County Highway F, Wisconsin Highway 77.

Travel season: Year-round. Roads may be ice-covered and slippery in winter months.

Camping: 85 sites at Interstate State Park, numerous private campgrounds along the way.

Services: Full services in the towns along the lower St. Croix, limited services in Trade River, Grantsburg, and Danbury along the upper St. Croix.

 The drive

The St. Croix River was born fifteen thousand years ago as raging meltwater from the retreating glacier. The water carved a deep channel through the land, leaving the river flanked by high bluffs.

Both the Ojibwe and Dakota tribes met the French trappers who came in search of beaver pelts in the early 1700s. Soon after the arrival of the

French, the Ojibwe drove the Dakota out of the area with French-supplied guns. The Dakota moved west into western and southern Minnesota. European fashion drove demand for beaver pelts. Changing tastes in Europe in the early 1800s, coupled with a steady decline in beaver populations from intense harvesting, brought an end to the fur trade era on the St. Croix. In 1834, the Ojibwe signed a treaty ceding most of the St. Croix watershed to the U.S. government. Logging replaced trapping as the area's main industry in the mid-1800s and drove the first big wave of white settlement in the area. The river and its tributaries floated millions of board feet of white pine to mills downstream. The boards that came out of these mills were shipped by rail to build cities and towns on the treeless great plains. Forests that once seemed inexhaustible were gone by the early 1900s, and the last log drive went down the St. Croix in 1914.

The drive begins at Mercord Mill Park in Prescott, overlooking the confluence of the Mississippi and St. Croix rivers. Prescott is named for Philander Prescott, who established a trading post and ferry across the St. Croix River here in 1839. To get to Mercord Mill Park, turn west on Orange Street from Broad Street/Wisconsin Highway 35. Orange Street is one block south of the bridge across the St. Croix River. Take a left after crossing the railroad tracks and you're there. If you look out into the middle of the water, you can see the line where the blue St. Croix meets the muddy Mississippi. The building at the park is the Prescott Bridge Gearhouse, which housed the motor and some of the gears that powered the original lift bridge across the St. Croix. The gearhouse was restored in 1991 by the Prescott Area Historical Society. It features photographs taken during construction of the lift bridge and is open to visitors Friday, Saturday, and Sunday afternoons from May to October.

Follow WI 35 north out of town. At the city limits, bear left where WI 35 divides from U.S. Highway 10. A mile later, take a left onto Pierce County F. The road rolls through upland farm country, and then dips down into the Kinnickinnic River valley. The entrance road to Kinnickinnic State Park is an immediate left at the northern crest of the valley; the turn pops up quickly, so be prepared. Kinnickinnic State Park's 1,242 acres contain 7 hiking trails through prairie and forest. Wildlife watchers can see bald eagles, osprey, wild turkeys, grey and red fox, as well as wood ducks, Canada geese, mink, and deer.

Continue on County F to Hudson and follow the signs for Interstate Highway 94. Take I-94 west for 1.5 miles and exit at Exit 1, just before the bridge over the St. Croix. You're now back on WI 35, headed into downtown Hudson. In 1852, the first mayor changed the city's name from Buena Vista to Hudson because the St. Croix reminded him of New York's Hudson River. Hudson grew with the lumber and steamboat industries in the 1850s and 1860s, and again with the railroads near the turn of the century. Hudson

Drive 12: St Croix River
Prescott to Riverside

MINNESOTA

St. Croix River

Riverside

Namekagon River

GOVERNOR KNOWLES STATE FOREST

CREX
MEADOWS
WILDLIFE
AREA

Ⓕ

77

Yellow River

70

Danbury

St. Croix River

FISH
LAKE
WILDLIFE
AREA

Gandy
Dancer
State Trail

35

87

WISCONSIN

8

INTERSTATE
STATE PARK

St. Croix Falls

Osceola

Apple River

35

Somerset

64

Willow River

Ⓘ

WILLOW RIVER
STATE PARK

Hudson

Ⓐ

To
St. Paul

KINNICKINNIC
STATE PARK

94

To
Eau Claire

Ⓕ

Kinnickinnic River

Prescott

10

Mississippi River

N

0   20   40

Miles

76

View of the St. Croix River Valley.

has an abundance of Victorian homes that date back to the 19th century; they can be found along Third and Fourth streets. Hudson's architectural heritage includes the eight-sided (and aptly named) Octagon House, built in 1845. The St. Croix County Historical Society purchased the Octagon House in 1964, and it is now open to the public as a museum. The house has been restored and furnished with authentic mid-Victorian period pieces. Two other buildings on the site contain a blacksmith shop, a country store, and various farm implements. The house is located at 1004 Third Street and open May through October, Tuesday through Sunday. WI 35 is the same as Hudson's Second Street. To find the house, turn right after passing through downtown, and then left onto Third Street.

Follow WI 35 north from Hudson to Somerset, which calls itself the "Tubing Capital of the World." Seemingly countless outfitters will be more than happy to put you in an old tractor tire inner tube and send you down the Apple River. Farther north on WI 35 is Osceola, orignially named Osceola Mills, nestled in the junction of the Osceola Creek and St. Croix River valleys. At the corner of First Avenue and Cascade Street, follow the wooden stairs to Cascade Falls.

Continue north on WI 35 to Interstate State Park, just south of the town of St. Croix Falls. Interstate State Park overlooks the Dalles of the St.

Croix River, formed when glacial meltwater cut a deep, vertical-walled gorge through the bedrock. These walls are popular with rock climbers today. Several trails provide excellent views of the glacial features in the park. The best views of the Dalles and glacial potholes are from the Pothole Trail, a short, 0.5-mile hike that follows the bluff above the narrowest part of the Dalles. Interstate's Pothole Trail is also the western terminus of the Ice Age Trail, a 1,000-mile hiking trail that winds along the kettle and terminal moraines of the Ice Age's last glacier. The park features the Ice Age Interpretive Center, near the park entrance, with excellent displays on Ice Age history and glacial landforms.

The Polk County Information Center, just north of the park entrance on WI 35, is the southern trailhead for the Gandy Dancer Trail. Running along 50 miles of abandoned Soo Line railroad track, the trail goes through nine towns and the forest and farmlands between them. The trail is open to hikers and mountain bikers. A bicycle pass is required; passes can be purchased at the Polk County Information Center, or in the towns along the way. Parking is available at many points along the trail, and as the segments range from 4.5 miles to 10 miles in length, it's great for day trips or extended journeys.

At the intersection of WI 35 and U.S. Highway 8, go under the overpass and follow US 8 west. Go about half a mile and take the first right onto Wisconsin Highway 87 into the town of St. Croix Falls. The falls today are hidden by a 60-foot Northern States Power hydroelectric dam. The river was originally dammed here by loggers to build a head of water to float logs over the falls and through the narrow Dalles to mills downriver. St. Croix Falls is home to the St. Croix National Scenic Riverway Headquarters, located just past the Johnson Feed Mill on the left side of the road. Headquarters staff are available to help travelers plan canoe trips along any part of the riverway. The headquarters also has displays on the river and its history.

Follow WI 87 north out of town, and you're off the beaten path. WI 87 is a smaller road than WI 35, with fewer towns and bigger curves. The scenery is wilder, the woods bigger, the traffic less. You'll pass through the unincorporated towns of Eureka Center, Cushing, and Trade River. North of Trade River, the farms run out and you enter a forest. This forest is older secondary growth of birch, oak, maple, and spruce, the forest that grew up after the white pines were clearcut during the logging era. North of Burnett County Highway O, on the left side of the road, is the Fish Lake Wildlife Area, a good place for wildlife viewing. For a side trip into the wildlife area, turn left onto County O. The pavement ends quickly, and the road is sand in some places, gravel in others. Turn right onto Stolte Road. You'll pass Dueholm Flowage, formed when the Logging Creek was dammed. Take another right on Fish Lake Road to get back to WI 87.

Just south of Grantsburg, there's a historical marker on the front lawn

Kinnickinnic River.

of the Bethany Lutheran Church commemorating Knute Anderson, founder of Grantsburg and known as the "Father of Burnett County" (perhaps as much for his twelve children as for his civic service). Grantsburg is at the intersection of WI 87 and Wisconsin Highway 70. This intersection has seen more than one ugly collision—look both ways twice. Go forward across WI 70, into town, and take a left on Main Street. Go down Main Street to Oak Street and take a right. Follow Oak Street for 0.75 mile and take a left, following signs for Crex Meadows Wildlife Area. You're now on Burnett County Highway F. Crex Meadows Wildlife Area is just north of Grantsburg on the right side of the road. Besides having great fishing, hunting, and wildlife viewing, Crex Meadows Wildlife Area is the center of the Crex Meadows Wolf Pack range. Keep your eyes and ears sharp, and you might see one of the northwoods's most elusive critters. Between Grantsburg and Danbury, County F wanders through the Crex Meadows Wildlife Area and along the border of the Governor Knowles State Forest. Governor Knowles State Forest has plenty of trees and solitude, as well as hiking and cross-country ski trails that flank the river through the length of the forest. County F is unpaved for about 2 miles between Grantsburg and Danbury; the ride is bumpy but passable for almost any vehicle.

County F ends at the intersection with Wisconsin Highway 77. Turn right on WI 77 and go into Danbury. In the middle of town, WI 77 intersects with WI 35. At the intersection, the Black Bear's Cave store sells great fudge. Turn left and follow WI 35/77 north. After 8 miles, WI 35 crosses the St. Croix, which ceases being the border river about a mile downstream from the bridge. At the bottom of the valley is Riverside Landing, a Burnett County Park and canoe landing, as well as the end of this drive and a great place for a picnic.

13

U.S. Highway 12

Black River Falls to Hudson

General description: This drive starts in Black River Falls and follows U.S. Highway 12 northwest to Willow River State Park, near Hudson. Both this drive and Drive 20 mostly run parallel to Interstate Highway 94, and both are laid-back alternatives to the high speed, semi-choked I-94 between Madison and Hudson. South of Black River Falls (Drive 20), US 12 parallels I-94 almost exactly. North of Black River Falls, I-94 cuts through part of the Driftless Area (the hilly, southwestern corner of the state untouched by Ice Age glaciers), but from Black River Falls to Eau Claire, US 12 runs east of I-94, following the eastern edge of the Driftless Area and running parallel to the Chicago & Northwestern Railroad track; it is an older path than I-94, and well-worn before the judicious use of TNT blasted a shorter trail through the Driftless Area hills.

Special attractions: Dells Mill Museum, Beaver Creek Reserve and Wise Nature Center, Eau Claire's Carson Park, Willow River State Park, camping, hiking, wildlife watching, canoeing, cross-country skiing.

Location: Western Wisconsin.

Drive route numbers: U.S. Highway 12, Wisconsin Highway 27, Eau Claire County Highways V and K, St. Croix County Highway U.

Travel season: Year-round.

Camping: 37 sites at Castle Mound Campground in the Black River State Forest, 72 sites at Willow River State Park, various county parks along the way.

Services: Full services in Black River Falls, Eau Claire, and Menomomie, limited elsewhere.

 The drive

Black River Falls is an old logging town. The area's first sawmill opened in 1839, and at the height of the logging era, fifty sawmills were turning logs into lumber in Jackson County. The Castle Mound Campground is located 1 mile south of Black River Falls on U.S. Highway 12, with 37 campsites, hiking and cross-country skiing trails, picnic area, and toilets.

As you head north out of Black River Falls on US 12, the road rolls

Drive 13: U.S. Highway 12
Black River Falls to Hudson

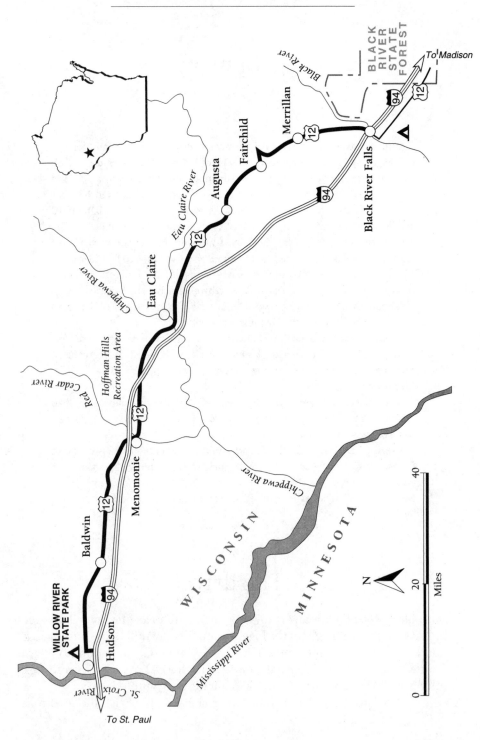

through bumpy, wooded hills. After a few miles, bluffs rise up on both sides of the road, and in the town of Merrillan, 11 miles from Black River Falls, you can see the waterfall that initially drew settlers here. Continue on US 12 for 11 miles to the junction with U.S. Highway 10, turn right onto US 10/12, and 2 miles farther, in the village of Fairchild, turn left to follow US 12 where it leaves US 10. Travel another 11 miles to Augusta.

In Augusta, the route leaves US 12 briefly. Turn right onto Wisconsin Highway 27, drive 3 miles, then turn left onto Eau Claire County Highway V and you'll come to the Dells Mill Museum, open from May 1 to October 31. The Dells Mill produced flour and livestock feed for more than a hundred years powered solely by its paddle wheel in Bridge Creek. Though only the five-story mill building remains today, a boarding house and school house once graced the mill property. This mill, like others in the state, was the site of constant activity from the middle of the nineteenth century to about 1910, when wheat was Wisconsin's chief cash crop. By 1900, milling was the second largest industry in the state (logging being first), but by 1920, most of the flour mills were abandoned; ninety years of bumper wheat crops had depleted the soil to the point that wheat would barely grow.

Continue west on County V for about a mile, turn right back onto US 12, and travel approximately 5 miles to Fall Creek. For a worthwhile side trip, travel 4 miles north of US 12 on Eau Claire County Highway K to the Beaver Creek Reserve and Wise Nature Center. The 360-acre reserve has 8 miles of hiking and cross-country skiing trails, self-guided interpretive trails, wildlife photography blinds, butterfly gardens, and boardwalks. The nature center features hands-on learning stations, interpretive displays, and live animal exhibits.

Back at US 12, travel 10 miles to Eau Claire ("clear water" in French). Go into town, and on the west side, follow the signs to 134-acre Carson park, home to the Paul Bunyan Logging Camp, the Chippewa Valley Museum, and a half-mile-long railroad. Open from April to Labor Day, the Paul Bunyan Logging Camp recreates an 1890s logging camp with a historic bunkhouse, cook's shanty, blacksmith shop, barn, logging equipment, and period artifacts, as well as an interpretive center with a movie, photographs, and lumbering artifacts. The Chippewa Valley Museum, open all year, tells the story of the peoples and history of the Chippewa Valley, including exhibits on the Ojibwe Indians, early towns and industries, and early farm life. The museum also houses a research library of local history, including more than ten thousand historic photographs, and on the grounds outside the museum, you'll find an 1850s log house and an 1880s one-room schoolhouse. If all that weren't enough, Carson Park is also home to the Chippewa Valley Railroad Association, which provides train rides through the park (Memorial Day through Labor Day) with coal-fired steam engines and an assortment of passenger coaches. The railroad is complete with a depot, round-

Willow Falls.

house, and switch yard.

As you head out of Eau Claire, US 12 is briefly a four-lane road. At the first stop light after you hit this freeway-like stretch, turn right to follow US 12, and then left at the first stop sign. Approximately 15 miles west of Eau Claire, you can try a 5-mile detour to Hoffman Hills State Recreation Area; it's a right turn onto Ney Road (follow the signs). Cross over I-94, go forward through the intersection with Dunn County Highway E, turn left after a very sharp corner and then right onto a gravel road. The 650-acre state recreation area offers 8 miles of quiet hiking trails, a 60-foot observation tower, and wildlife viewing, but no camping.

Continue west on US 12 to Menomonie. The Knapp, Stout & Company's lumbering operations dominated the Menomonie economy during the logging years, paying its workers not in dollars but in company-issued money called "scrip," which was redeemable at the company store. This worked out well for the company, as it was able to turn a profit on the "money" with which it "paid" its workers—annual sales at Knapp, Stout & Company general stores approached $750,000. The Dunn County Heritage Museum on 7th and Wilson Avenues, open June to September, traces human history from prehistoric times through Native American history to the logging era and the present day. The 106-year-old Mabel Tainter Memorial Theater on Main Street, open all year, is a magnificent example of Victorian-era architecture and interior design, with hand-stenciled walls and ceiling; carved mahogany, walnut and oak woodwork; a marble staircase, and ornate fireplaces. US 12 makes a few turns as it winds through Menomonie. At the first stoplight in town, bear right. In the middle of town, watch for US 12 to turn left; and approximately 1 mile after you cross the Red Cedar River, US 12 turns right.

For the 25 miles from Menomonie to Hammond, US 12 winds pleasantly through wooded hills. This area, like the Driftless Area to the south, was untouched by the last wave of glaciation, but unlike the Driftless Area, it was covered by a glacier at one point during the Ice Age. The rolling upland here is not as steep nor as dry as the Driftless Area, and neither is it as wet as the land to the north. At the stop sign in Baldwin, at the junction with U.S. Highway 63, turn right, and then just after you pass through town, turn left to continue west on US 12. Travel 3 miles to Hammond, and turn right at the stop sign. West of Hammond, the hills are smaller with fewer trees, the land mostly given to corn fields and pastures.

Approximately 13 miles out of Hammond, a right on St. Croix County Highway U will take you to the end of this drive, Willow River State Park. The park was created in the early 1970s when Northern States Power, the utility that supplies electricity and gas to much of the region, donated 3 hydroelectric dams and 1,300 acres to the state of Wisconsin. The park contains both the Willow River Gorge and the surrounding uplands. Seven trails take hikers over glacial deposits and through the Willow River Gorge to Willow Falls. To get to Willow Falls, park in the lot near the park office and head down the Pioneer Trail. You'll find the falls after about 0.5 mile. The park features seventy-two campsites, a swimming beach, amphitheater, picnic area, and canoe rental.

To get to I-94 from the park, travel back the way you came on County U, turn right onto US 12 and travel just over a mile to the freeway entrance ramp.

14

Great River Road Part I

Prescott to La Crosse

General description: The Great River Road (so named in 1938) follows the Mississippi River from its headwaters at Lake Itasca, Minnesota, to the Gulf of Mexico. Marked by signs showing green steamboat wheels on a white background, this drive follows Wisconsin Highway 35 and the Great River Road from Prescott to La Crosse, 125 miles south. The river is flanked on both sides by high, rugged bluffs, and dotted with bluff-side towns. Along the way you will learn some of the ancient landmarks that have guided Mississippi River travelers for centuries.

Special attractions: Lake Pepin, the world's largest six-pack, Laura Ingalls Wilder's birthplace, Trempealeau National Wildlife Refuge, Perrot State Park, camping, fishing, hiking, biking, cross-country skiing, wildlife watching.

Location: Western Wisconsin, along the border with Minnesota from Prescott to La Crosse.

Drive route numbers: Wisconsin Highway 35.

Travel season: Year-round. Spring and fall are best for migratory bird watching.

Camping: 97 sites at Perrot State Park, 12 sites at Rieck's Lake Park, various private enterprises along the way.

Services: Full services in La Crosse, limited elsewhere. Restaurants and bed & breakfasts are found in most of the towns on the route.

 The drive

The Mississippi River has long been a travel and transport route—Native Americans and French fur traders paddled the river in their canoes, and steamboats brought goods and settlers. In 1930, Congress directed the Army Corps of Engineers to develop and maintain a 9-foot-deep, 400-foot-wide navigation channel on the Upper Mississippi between St. Louis, Missouri, and St. Paul, Minnesota. The Corps built a system of twenty-nine locks and dams to regulate water flow and maintain the 9-foot-channel. Roughly 175 million tons of freight is pushed up and down the Upper

Drive 14: Great River Road Part 1
Prescott to La Crosse

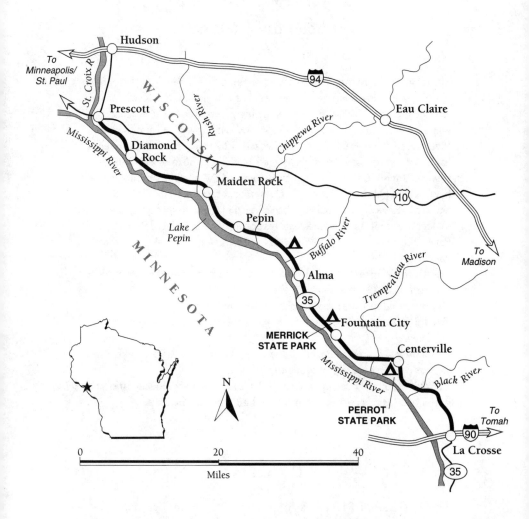

Mississippi each year, mostly grain heading south to New Orleans, while petroleum products from Louisiana and Texas oil fields and coal from Kentucky come north. One river-barge has a 1,500-ton capacity, the equivalent of 15 railroad cars or 58 semi-trailer trucks. Typical tows contain 12 to 15 barges, carrying as much as 45 million pounds of bulk freight.

The drive begins at the confluence of the Mississippi and St. Croix rivers, at Mercord Mill Park in Prescott. To get to Mercord Mill Park, turn west on Orange Street from Broad Street/Wisconsin Highway 35, 1 block south of the bridge across the St. Croix River. Take a left after crossing the railroad tracks. The line where the muddy Mississippi meets the blue St. Croix is clearly visible from the park. The Prescott Bridge Gearhouse, restored in 1991, features photographs taken during construction of the lift bridge that spanned the river here, and is open to visitors Friday, Saturday, and Sunday afternoons from May to October.

Travel south from Prescott on WI 35. Outside of Prescott, the road runs near the bottom of the Mississippi valley, with the Diamond Bluffs in the near distance. The road then climbs out of the valley and winds through forested uplands before returning to the valley at the village of Diamond Bluff, 13 miles from Prescott. South of Diamond Bluff, the road parallels the Burlington Northern Railroad track along the base of the bluff.

About 6 miles out of Diamond Bluff, a historical marker on the left side of the road points out an arrangement of boulders on the bluff behind the sign. In 1902, archaeologist Jacob Brower interpreted the arrangement as a represention of a bow and arrow, drawn to shoot toward Lake Pepin, to the southeast. The age, origin, and meaning of this possibly ancient landmark remain a mystery.

Bay City, 10 miles south of Diamond Bluff, sits at the head of Lake Pepin. Several thousand years ago, glacial debris washed down the Chippewa River and blocked the Mississippi channel, backing up the river and creating 22-mile-long Lake Pepin. Varying from 1 to 2.5 miles in width, the bluff-bound lake is especially beautiful at sunset. As you continue south from Bay City, the road rolls up to the top of the bluff.

Maiden Rock, perched on the bluff above the lake, takes its name from a Dakota Indian legend about a girl forced to marry against her will. Her relatives sent away the young man she loved, and though she held out for a year, they eventually saw her married to a man of their choosing at the top of the bluff just south of town. An hour after the ceremony she was missing, and in the morning they found her broken body at the base of the bluff. A turn-out and scenic overlook on the right side of the road marks the site of her doom with picnic tables and toilets.

Travel 13 miles from Maiden Rock to Pepin, birthplace of Laura Ingalls Wilder, author of the classic *Little House* books. For a quick side trip to the farm where Wilder was born, complete with a replica of the log cabin Wilder

Maiden Rock.

describes in *Little House in the Big Woods*, turn left onto Pepin County High-way CC, about a mile before Pepin, and travel 7 miles to the Little House Wayside. In Pepin, the Historical Museum features local history and exhib-its on Wilder. She was born on February 7, 1867, and waited to write about her childhood experiences until she was sixty-five. She wrote eight immensely popular books before her death in 1957.

As you continue south on WI 35 from Pepin, you soon cross the Chippewa River and travel through the 12,500-acre Tiffany Bottoms Wild-life Area. When you get into Nelson, turn left to follow WI 35—you will know you missed this turn if you cross the river. South of Nelson, the rough-hewn bluffs stick out like noses into the valley.

Rieck's Lake Park is found where the Buffalo River joins the Missis-sippi, 7 miles south of Nelson. The park has twelve campsites along the lake (they fill up quickly), and observation decks offer views of migratory water-fowl such as tundra swans, Canada geese, and many varieties of ducks, as well as bald eagles, osprey, and turkey vultures.

Alma, 2 miles south of the park, is squeezed onto a narrow strip of land between the river and Twelve Mile Bluff. The village is only 2 streets wide, but 7 miles long. Lock and Dam #4 stretches across the river near the center of town. At Buena Vista City Park, 500 feet above the river, you can see for miles and stand where eagles soar. To get there, turn left onto Buffalo County Highway E, and then left again at the sign to the park, and then left again another half-mile later.

The sixty-seven-site campground at Merrick State Park, 15 miles south of Alma, lies on an island in the Mississippi River. There is a beach, a picnic area, and good wildlife watching. At Fountain City, 12 miles beyond Merrick Park, you can enjoy watching the river traffic at Lock and Dam #5.

Established in 1936 by President Franklin D. Roosevelt, the Trempealeau National Wildlife Refuge, 10 miles south of Fountain City, is 706 acres set aside as a refuge and breeding ground for migratory birds and other wildlife. A 5-mile wildlife drive takes you through the sand prairie, marsh, and hardwood forest habitats. Four nature trails take hikers to the highlights of the refuge, and biking is permitted on all refuge roads. Spring and fall are the best times to see great blue herons, geese, and ducks. The 24-mile Great River State Trail runs through the refuge on an abandoned Chicago and Northwestern Railroad grade.

Continue on WI 35 to Centerville, and turn right in the middle of town to follow the Great River Road. South of Centerville, Perrot State Park occupies the site where Nicholas Perrot, the reputedly dark and handsome French trader and diplomat, had his winter camp at the base of Trempealeau Mountain. Perrot built a fort at Prairie du Chien in early 1685, moved north, spent the winter here, and then moved on to build another fort on Lake Pepin. The 384-foot Trempealeau Mountain has been a landmark for

Lake Pepin.

centuries. It was called *La Montagne qui trempe a l'eau* ("The Mountain which is steeped in the water") by the French. The local Dakota considered the mountain sacred; burial and ceremonial mounds dot the park.

At the intersection with U.S. Highway 53, WI 35 turns right and joins US 53 South and then exits again 2 miles later. Continue on WI 35 into La Crosse, which got its name from the French name that fur traders gave to the game played in the 1700s by Native Americans on the prairies that stretched east from the Mississippi to the bluffs (basically downtown La Crosse today). The game was played with a ball and long-handled rackets, similar to those used for lacrosse today. Beer became a major influence in the local economy in the late 1800s, and at one point seven breweries cranked out the local brew. Only one remains today, the G. Heileman Brewery (recently purchased by Stroh's) on South Third Street, home of the world's largest six-pack. Grandad Bluff towers over 500 feet above the city and offers views of the city and both Minnesota and Iowa across the river. The first week in October is not only a great time to see the fall colors along the river, it's also time for Oktoberfest, and all the beer, sauerkraut, and wiener schnitzel you can stomach.

From La Crosse, you can easily continue on to Drive16, which continues on the Great River Road from La Crosse to Dubuque, Iowa.

15

The Driftless Area
Trempealeau County

General description: This route runs like a roller-coaster ride through the heart of the Driftless Area, the hilly southwestern corner untouched by the glaciers that scraped across the rest of the state. This rolling upland is a maze of interconnecting valleys cut by countless trout streams. Each hilltop provides spectacular views and every valley is dotted with red barns, corn fields, and quietly grazing cows. The farms here are small, each farmer's space defined as much by the valley as the fenceposts. It's an area unsuited to mammoth corporate farming operations.

Special attractions: The most scenic hill-top views per mile of any drive in this book, Amish country, fishing, hiking, skiing.

Location: Western Wisconsin.

Drive route numbers: Wisconsin Highways 54 and 95, Jackson County Highway D, Trempealeau County Highways D and S, U.S. Highway 53.

Travel season: Year-round.

Camping: 37 sites at Castle Mound State Forest Campground, 21 sites at Crystal Lake Campground, camping at Blair Memorial Park.

Services: Check the fluids in Black River Falls. Limited services in Whitehall, spotty elsewhere.

 ## The drive

This drive begins in Black River Falls, which began as a logging town. The area's first sawmill opened in 1839, and at the height of the logging era, fifty sawmills were turning logs into lumber in Jackson County. The falls from which the town draws its name was harnessed long ago to turn the blades of the mills, but where Wisconsin Highway 54 crosses the river in the middle of town, the river is still rocky and lined by the white pines that initially brought lumberjacks to the area. The Castle Mound State Forest campground, 1 mile south of town on U.S. Highway 12, has 37 campsites, great hiking and cross-country skiing trails leading through wooded hills, and a picnic area.

Travel southwest on WI 54, and you're headed straight into the Driftless Area in the Black River valley, with river bluffs etched out of the hills on

Drive 15: The Driftless Area
Trempealeau County

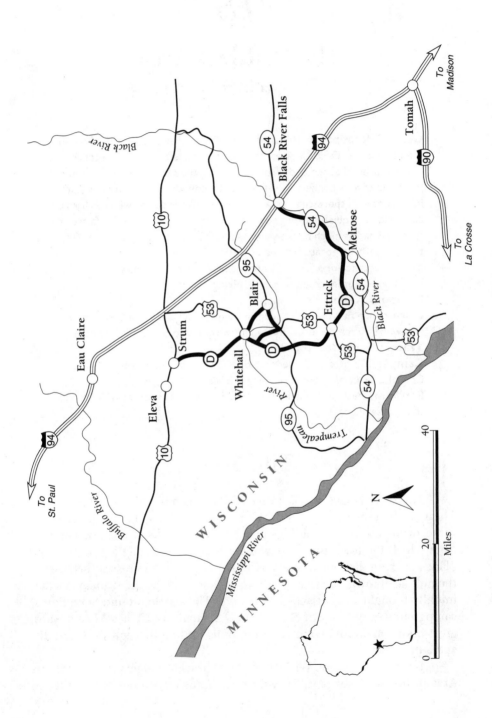

either side of the road. It's romantic country—I once got engaged while driving this route (it didn't take). Approximately 14 miles out of Black River Falls, turn right onto Jackson County Highway D. If you come to the town of Melrose, you've gone too far.

The hills are steep and frequent, topped by both hardwoods and pines. The valleys are marshy, and the dark wetland soil supports an abundance of corn, which mostly goes to feed the dairy cows. Roughly 8 miles from WI 54, just after the intersection with Jackson County Highway V, the road enters Trempealeau County and follows Trempealeau County D northwest to Strum, the end of the drive. The road itself is rough in spots—paved but potholed, often narrow, always twisting, and sometimes without a centerline.

Approximately 15 miles along County D from WI 54 is the village of Ettrick, named after the Ettrick Forest in the Scottish Highlands. As you come into Ettrick, you're traveling along the floor of the valley of the South Fork of Beaver Creek. Once you get into town, watch for County D to turn left and, 2 blocks later, go forward at the intersection with U.S. Highway 53. County D then climbs the steep valley wall and rolls along the top of a winding line of hills for a couple of miles before descending again, this time into the French Creek Valley, near the intersection with Trempealeau County T. County D traces French Creek through the valley, back to its beginning, and heads up the hillside again. County D then dips down into the Lake Coulee Creek Valley, crosses the creek, and goes up again.

At the intersection with Wisconsin Highway 95, go forward. It's not a Speed Racer course in the least, and for most of the drive on County D, I didn't need more than three gears. If the person in front of you is going too slowly, pull over, let them get ahead of you, and enjoy the magnificent scenery; you won't get the chance to pass. There isn't a single passing zone on the whole length of Trempealeau County D. Beyond WI 95, County D continues through the hills until it reaches Irvin Creek and follows the creek to its confluence with the Trempealeau River at Whitehall.

European settlers began farming these valleys in the 1850s. Whitehall was born as a railroad town in 1873 when the Green Bay and Western Railroad laid down its tracks along the Trempealeau River. The tracks followed the twisting Trempealeau from its mouth at the Mississippi River to its source just on the other side of the Driftless Area, using the river's valley as a trail through the steep, train-defying hills. Whitehall is now the seat of Trempealeau County. County D joins US 53 North in Whitehall; travel north through town on County D/US 53.

There is a large Amish settlement to the east of Whitehall. The Amish are descendedants of a group of Swiss who held beliefs different from those of the official Swiss state church in the seventeenth century. They believed that baptism at birth led to mere lip service in faith, and thus one should not be baptised until early adulthood. They obeyed the Biblical command "To

River valley in the Driftless Area.

this world do not conform," and lived a simple, plain existence without luxuries. On January 21, 1625, the members of the group were rebaptised, dubbed themselves Anabaptists (they were also known as Swiss Brethren and later as Mennonites, after one of their early leaders, Menno Simmons), and broke away from the state church. Finding this an excellent excuse to reinstitute public burnings, the state church wasted no time rounding up the Brethren and using them to light the village squares at night. Finding this treatment less than appealing, the Anabaptists scattered across Europe and worshipped in their homes for fear of persecution—today the Amish still worship in their homes. In 1693, Jacob Amman decided that the high-living Mennonites were too worldly and started a stricter sect with a small group of followers, later called Amish after their leader. Amish started arriving in America in search of religious freedom in the 1700s, and a few of them settled in the fertile, secluded valleys of Trempealeau County in the 1800s.

Outside of Whitehall, the route goes in a loop through Amish country. Follow US 53 northeast out of town for approximately 2 miles and turn right onto Trempealeau County Highway S. About 1 mile down County S, you can see one of the schools where Amish children study the three Rs in grades 1-8. Amish children start school at age six and finish at age fourteen. The kitchen is usually the largest room, and is the center of the Amish home. In the spring and fall, you can see the Amish working their fields with horses and manual equipment, the same way their forebears did a hundred years ago. Many Amish have taken up crafts and trades in addition to farming, and many of them sell their wares in shops in this area. You're likely to have more success in any dealings with the Amish if you dress conservatively and leave your camera in the car.

Turn right onto WI 95 and travel west to Blair, which has camping at the Blair Memorial Park on Lake Henry. Follow WI 95 where it joins up with US 53, and where WI 95 and US 53 diverge, follow US 53 north along the Trempealeau River into Whitehall. Continue through Whitehall on US 53, then turn left onto County D just north of town. The road here is narrow and lacks a shoulder. Turn left at the junction with Trempealeau County Highway E and travel along Elk Creek for about 1 mile, then turn right with County D and follow the fairly straight Bruce Valley Creek. You'll notice that the hills are mellower here, the roads straighter, the farms larger and closer together. This is the extreme northern part of the Driftless Area, and it was glaciated at one point, unlike the land to the south. The last wave of glaciation, which ended about twelve thousand years ago, advanced and retreated over a good length of the state twice, both times skirting the state's southwest region. This area was glaciated the first time, but not the second, and the hills here are not nearly as steep as those further south.

A church spire rises above County D in the Driftless Area. FRANCINE CIESLICKI PHOTO

At the junction with Trempealeau County Highway OO, turn left, and at the junction with Trempealeau County H, turn left again and head into Strum, the end of this drive. Turn right at the stop sign in Strum. Crystal Lake, near the intersection with Highway 10 on the north side of town, was created by damming the Buffalo River, and today offers trout, bass, and walleye fishing, as well as a swimming beach and twenty-one wooded campsites.

From Strum, I-94 is 9 miles east on U.S. Highway 10. Or, if for no other reason than that there's a story about its name, head west on US 10 to Eleva. It seems the town was originally called New Chicago. Soon after the town was founded, the founders decided to have the word "ELEVATOR" painted on the grain elevator next to the railroad tracks. The painters got started late in the season, and by the time the snow was flying and it was too cold to paint, they had only painted "ELEVA". They never did finish the job, and the town ended up renamed.

16

Great River Road Part II
La Crosse to Dickeyville

General description: This 120-mile drive follows the Mississippi River from La Crosse to Dickeyville, rolling past magnificent river bluffs and corn-filled upland prairies. Much of the length of the river along this drive is protected as the Upper Mississippi River Wildlife and Fish Refuge. The refuge includes 200,000 acres of riverbottom land (from Wabasha, Minnesota, to Rock Island, Illinois) set aside to protect migratory birds and native wildlife. Eagles and osprey soar above the bluffs, and all manner of wild critters frolic in the many parks and preserves along the way.

Special attractions: Blackhawk Recreation Area, Wyalusing State Park, Nelson Dewey State Park, St. John Lead Mine, Dickeyville Grotto, camping, hiking, biking, fishing, wildlife watching.

Location: Southwestern Wisconsin.

Drive route numbers: Wisconsin Highways 35 and 133, Grant County Highways C, X, A, VV.

Travel season: Year-round.

Camping: 132 sites at Wyalusing State Park, 73 sites at the Grant River Recreation area, various private campgrounds along the way.

Services: Full services in La Crosse and Prairie du Chien.

 The drive

This drive starts in La Crosse, the name French fur traders gave to the game played in the 1700s by Native Americans on the prairies stretching east from the Mississippi to the bluffs (basically downtown La Crosse today). The game was played with a ball and long-handled rackets, precursor to the modern game of lacrosse. Permanent settlement in the area began in 1841, when Nathan Myrick built a cabin here and began trading with the local Winnebago Indians. Mississippi River shipping and lumbering first spurred commerce in La Crosse, which was incorporated as a city in 1856 with a population of 745. When both river traffic and white pine dwindled in the late 1800s, local residents of German descent began brewing beer, and at one point seven breweries cranked out their brews. Only one remains

Drive 16: Great River Road Part II
La Crosse to Dickeyville

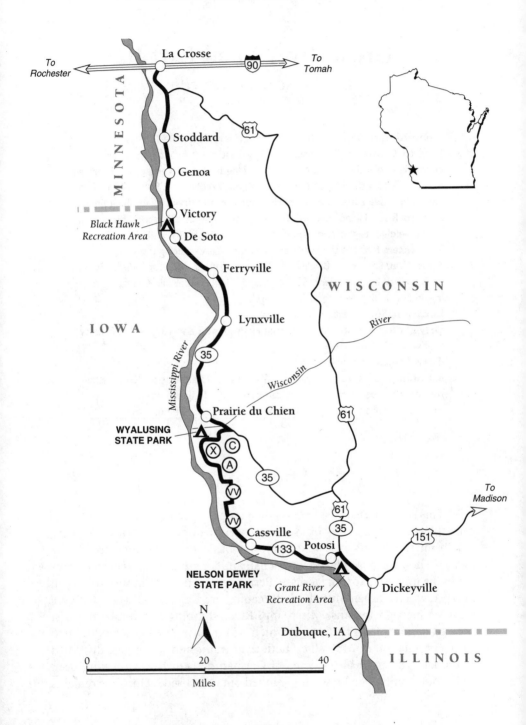

today—the G. Heileman Brewery (recently purchased by Stroh's) on South Third Street, home of the world's largest six-pack. The brewery is open for tours year-round. Grandad Bluff towers more than 500 feet above La Crosse and offers views of the city and Minnesota (and on a clear day, Iowa, to the far southwest) across the river; to get there, follow Main Street east out of downtown. The first week in October is not only a great time to see the fall colors along the river, it's also time for Oktoberfest and all the beer, sauerkraut, and wiener schnitzel you can stomach.

Drive south on Wisconsin Highway 35 from La Crosse. Two miles south of town is Goose Island County Park, which is spread over several islands in the Mississippi. The park has more than 400 campsites, a beach, a boat launch, a picnic area, and 6 miles of hiking and cross-country skiing trails. As you continue south on WI 35, you'll see many places to pull over and watch both wildlife and river traffic.

Stoddard, 11 miles south of La Crosse, wasn't a Mississippi River town until Lock and Dam #8 was built at Genoa (another 6 miles south of Stoddard), flooding 18,000 acres of river bottom and making it a much shorter walk between Main Street and the beach. Approximately 3 miles south of Genoa, you'll cross the Bad Axe River, which has lent its name to two battles between Winnebago and U.S. troops. The first, fought June 28, 1827, between a small force of Winnebago and the crew of a river boat, is memorialized on a stone marker along the road. The second, fought August 1–2, 1832, ended the Black Hawk War.

In April of 1832, one thousand Sauk Indians led by their chief, Black Hawk, crossed the Mississippi River from Iowa to reclaim their homeland from European settlers near present-day Sauk City (Drive 17). Black Hawk succeeded in bringing his people back to their land, but was soon on the run back to Iowa, chased by the U.S. Army. The army contacted Fort Crawford in Prairie du Chien, and when Black Hawk and his people got to the river, they found themselves trapped between the pursuing army and an armed steamboat on the river. The Sauk Indians plunged into the river—most were shot or drowned, and some were taken prisoner.

Three hundred Sauk somehow made the crossing. Waiting on the far side of the river was a force of Dakota Indians who had been recruited to help the army by General Atkinson, and half of the Sauk that made the crossing lost their lives in that fighting. At the battle's end, only 150 of the 1,000 Sauk who began the journey in April had lived to tell the tale. Black Hawk himself was captured and imprisoned at Fort Crawford. Abraham Lincoln, Jefferson Davis, and Zachary Taylor all served in the Black Hawk War as young officers. The Black Hawk Recreation Area, 1.5 miles south of Victory, is named in remembrance of the second Battle of Bad Axe, and has riverfront campsites, a picnic area, and a beach.

Wisconsin River, Wyalusing State Park.

De Soto, named for the Spanish explorer who first stumbled onto the Mississippi River, is 4 miles south of Victory. It was built on a Native American cemetery, and local legend has it that the first Chief Winneshiek, of the Winnebago, is buried here. The Winnebago fought on the British side during the War of 1812, chiefly because they were enemies of the Ojibwe, who were allied with the French after years of mutually profitable fur trading. Winneshiek and his troops helped the British capture Fort Shelby at Prairie du Chien from the U.S. The second Winnebago chief named Winneshiek was removed with his tribe to the west, but later returned to Wisconsin to settle near Black River Falls (Drives 14, 15, 16, and 22).

Ferryville, 8 miles south of De Soto, had its humble beginnings under the name of "Humble Bush," but got its current name when ferry service across the Mississippi was established here in the nineteenth century. Another 8 miles down the road is Lynxville, where the largest raft of white pine logs ever to grace the Mississippi was assembled and floated south in 1896, containing roughly 2.25 million board feet of lumber and measuring 1550 feet long by 270 feet wide. The town's name was taken from the Lynx, the steamboat that brought the first surveyors to the area. Before the installation of the lock and dam system, Lynxville had an excellent harbor, and it became one of the stopping points for river boats traveling between St. Louis, Missouri, and St. Paul, Minnesota.

Travel another 15 miles south to Prairie du Chien, the second oldest European settlement in the state (Green Bay being the oldest). The town is named for a Fox chief whose name, *Alim*, translates to "Dog" in English. The French fur traders named the area "Prairie of the Dog," or *Prairie du Chien*. When Europeans arrived in the seventeenth century, the prairie near the mouth of the Wisconsin River was considered neutral territory by Native Americans, and as many as fourteen different tribes either lived in the region or visited for trade. Nicholas Perrot found the area an excellent place to establish a fur trading depot in the 1680s, and a few more white settlers arrived in the 1770s. During the War of 1812, American troops built Fort Shelby here, only to have it captured and destroyed by the the British and Chief Winneshiek's Winnebagos in the same year it was built, 1814. In 1816, when the war was over, the U.S. Army built Fort Crawford a short distance from the site of Fort Shelby, and rebuilt it in 1829. The Fort Crawford Medical Museum at 717 South Beaumont Road is housed in the old Fort Crawford Military Hospital. On St. Feriole Island, you'll find Villa Louis, open May 1 through October 31, once the home of the Hercules Dousman family and now a museum of Victorian decorative arts. Dousman arrived here in 1826 and built Villa Louis after amassing considerable sums of money in the fur trade. The island also features a fur trade museum, burial mounds, log cabins, and the ruins of the first Fort Crawford.

The route continues on WI 35 south from Prairie du Chien across the Wisconsin River, then turns right onto Grant County Highway C towards Wyalusing State Park. At the intersection with Grant County Highway X, turn right and travel approximately 1 mile to the park entrance. *Wyalusing* is a Munsee-Delaware Indian term meaning "home of the warrior." The area has been inhabited by a variety of peoples since the retreat of Wisconsin's glaciers eleven thousand years ago. One of these groups was the Effigy Mound Builders, who left twenty-five mounds here. A group of nine mounds is easily accessible on the Sentinel Ridge Nature Trail, a 0.5 mile loop starting at the Green Cloud Picinic Area. Point Lookout provides great views of the intersecting valleys of the Wisconsin and Mississippi rivers, and if you head down the trail to your left, then turn right onto Cave Trail, you'll soon come to a set of steep wooden steps that lead up to a cave in the bluff. The park has 22 miles of hiking trails that wander past caves and Indian mounds, along the bluffs and through hardwood forests, as well as a 132-site campground, canoeing trail, and cross-country skiing.

Back in your car, turn right out of the park onto County X. When County X ends at a stop sign in Bagley, turn left onto Grant County Highway A. After a few miles, the Great River Road turns right onto Grant County Highway VV and rolls past upland prairie farms. Turn right at the intersection with Grant County Highway V, then left about a mile later to follow County VV, and you're back to the bluffs.

A few miles from County V you come to Nelson Dewey State Park and the Stonefield State Historic Site. Nelson Dewey was the first governor of the state of Wisconsin and Stonefield was his farm. Stonefield today is a museum of agricultural history and village life of the late nineteenth century, with a complete village including shops, train depot, and saloon. The agricultural museum features historic farm implements, including a full-size threshing machine.

Continue south on County VV to Cassville, where County VV ends. Turn right onto Wisconsin Highway 133 and travel 19 miles past prairie farms to Potosi. The Grant River Recreation Area, offering seventy-three campsites, hiking, fishing, a boat launch, a playground, horseshoe pits, volleyball nets, and basketball courts, appears just before you get to Potosi. On Main Street in Potosi you'll find the St. John Mine, which began as a natural cave and was mined extensively by Native Americans. The discovery of lead in the region brought the first great wave of European settlement to the state in 1828. Willis St. John was the first non-Native American to work the mine, and he made a small fortune in twenty years of mining. Tours of the mine are offered May 1 through November 1.

Continue on WI 133 for 1 mile, turn right onto WI 35/U.S. Highway 61, and travel 8 miles to Dickeyville, the end of this drive. Father Matthias Werner built the Dickeyville Grotto here, an eclectic collection of sculpture and structures built from stone, mortar, and such things as colored glass, petrified wood, pottery shards, sea shells, fossils, agate, quartz, and onyx. You really have to see it to appreciate it—it's an experience. Nearly ten thousand people attended its dedication in 1930, and it continues to attract a large number of visitors today.

From here, U.S. Highway 151 North will take you to Madison, or continue on WI 35 to get to Dubuque, Iowa.

17

The Lower Wisconsin River
Frank Lloyd Wright and Ancient Sites

General description: This 100-mile drive follows the Lower Wisconsin River from its confluence with the Mississippi River at Wyalusing State Park to Sauk City. The river has cut a deep, bluff-lined valley through the hilly Driftless Area, the southwestern part of the state untouched by the last Ice Age glaciers. The river is wide, with many sandbars and shifting channels, and many a wildlife refuge protects its banks. The route runs through the river valley, detouring occasionally for such things as a tour of Frank Lloyd Wright history and architecture and Natural Bridge State Park, where evidence of the oldest human habitation in the Midwest was found beneath a shelter of overhanging rock.

Special attractions: Wyalusing State Park, Kickapoo Indian Caverns, Frank Lloyd Wright's birthplace, home, and assorted architectural works, Natural Bridge State Park, camping, hiking, biking, canoeing.

Location: Southwestern Wisconsin.

Drive route numbers: Grant County Highways C and X, Wisconsin Highways 35, 60, and 80, U.S. Highway 14, Sauk County Highways B and C.

Travel season: Year-round.

Camping: 132 sites at Wyalusing State Park, various private enterprises along the way.

Services: Full services in Prairie du Chien (north of the start of the drive on WI 35), limited elsewhere.

 **The drive**

This drive starts at Wyalusing State Park, overlooking the confluence of the Wisconsin and Mississippi rivers. Find the park by turning west onto Grant County Highway C from Wisconsin Highway 35. When the first Europeans arrived in the seventeenth century, the land around the mouth of the Wisconsin River was considered neutral territory by Native Americans, and as many as fourteen different tribes either lived in the region or visited for trade. *Wyalusing* is a Munsee-Delaware Indian term meaning "home of the warrior." The area has been inhabited by a variety of peoples since the retreat of Wisconsin's glaciers eleven thousand years ago; one of these groups

Drive 17: The Lower Wisconsin River
Frank Lloyd Wright and Ancient Sites

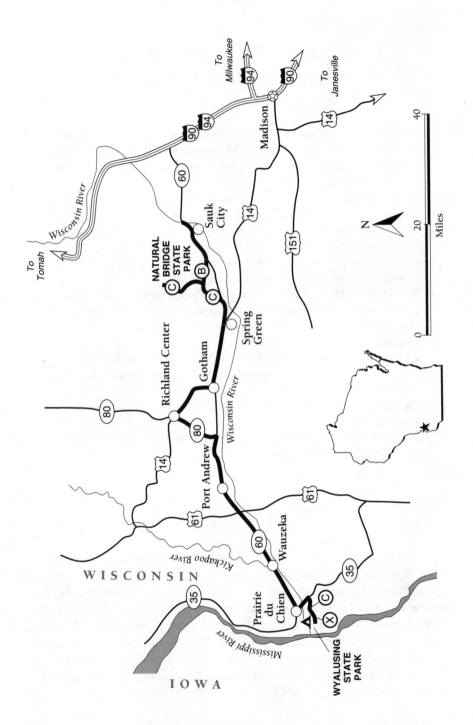

Natural Bridge in Natural Bridge State Park.

was the Effigy Mound Builders, who left twenty-five mounds here. A group of nine mounds is easily accessible on the Sentinel Ridge Nature Trail, a 0.5 mile loop starting from the Green Cloud Picinic Area. The park has 22 miles of hiking trails that wander past caves and indian mounds, along the bluffs and through hardwood forests, as well as a 132-site campground, canoeing trail, and cross-country skiing.

Back at WI 35, turn left and cross the river, then turn right onto Wisconsin Highway 60. Approximately 9 miles from the WI 35/WI 60 intersection, you'll see signs for the Kickapoo Indian Caverns, open May 15 through October 31. The caverns's many chambers were long a shelter to local Native Americans and are the state's largest subterranean feature. The caverns were brought to the attention of European settlers by miners in the 1880s. The caverns now house a museum of artifacts found in the caves from several Native American cultures.

Continue on WI 60 another 2 miles to Wauzeka. The origin of the town's name is a subject of local debate. One story claims the town is named for Wauzega, who, in the nineteenth century, exiled himself from his tribe and settled with his wife here at the mouth of the Kickapoo River, and was presumably around to meet European settlers. Another story says the town is named for Wauzeegah, the son of a Fox chief and a Winnebago woman, who brought his family here in the seventeenth century. Yet another says the name derives from Wisaka, a god of the Kickapoo Indians. Whatever the case, the town was incorporated as Wauzeekaw in 1857, and the name has since been shortened to its current form. In Wauzeka, watch for the signs as WI 60 turns first left, then right. Approximately 2 miles east of Wauzeka, you'll cross the Kickapoo River just north of its confluence with the Wisconsin River. The winding Kickapoo is a great canoeing river—while it's only 33 miles long through Crawford County as the crow flies, the many twists and turns make for more than 100 river-miles of canoeing.

About 10 miles east of Wauzeka, WI 60 joins U.S. Highway 61 for 1 mile, and then WI 60 turns right and continues along the Wisconsin River. In another 8 miles you reach Port Andrew, site of Richland County's oldest homestead. Once a busy river town, Port Andrew's fortunes waned when the railroad track was laid on the other side of the river, and Blue River, opposite Port Andrew on the south side of the river, was established as a railroad town. As river traffic lessened and the railroads became the preferred method of shipping everything from timber to goods to settlers, Port Andrew quickly declined.

Approximately 10 miles east of Port Andrew, turn left onto Wisconsin Highway 80 and travel 9 miles north to Richland Center, where architect Frank Lloyd Wright was born in 1867. Wright returned here after World War I to design the A. D. German Warehouse. Some say the four-story structure, which is open for public tours, resembles a Mayan temple because of its narrow vertical windows and the concrete frieze around the top floor. The town celebrates its most famous hometown boy during the first weekend in June with tours, carriage rides, and lectures on Wright's life and works. Turn right onto U.S. Highway 14 in Richland Center and travel 10 miles to Gotham. Continue on US 14 through Gotham. On your left along the 5-mile stretch between Gotham and Lone Rock, buttes and river bluffs rise sharply from the river's flat floodplain. You'll also find the Lone Rock unit of the Lower Wisconsin State Riverway, with trails and wildlife viewing along the river.

Continue another 7 miles to Spring Green, turn right onto Wisconsin Highway 23, and travel south into town. Spring Green was born as a railroad village when the Milwaukee and Mississippi Rail Line came through in 1856. Frank Lloyd Wright spent his boyhood summers at his uncle's farm just south of town, and in 1911, Wright returned to Spring Green to build his home, Taliesin, at the junction of WI 23 and Iowa County Highway C on the south side of the river. From 1911 to his death in 1959, Wright modified and experimented with the 6 structures he built on the 600-acre property, including the Romeo and Juliet Windmill, Hillside Home School (now the Hillside School for Architects), Midway Farm, River View Terrace (now the Frank Lloyd Wright Visitor Center), and Taliesin. The Spring Green area is also rich with the work of Wright's students, with many low, flat-roofed buildings built with prominent horizontal lines in the style that Wright

A county highway heads for the bluffs.

pioneered.

Head back to US 14/WI 60, turn right, and then left where US 14 and WI 60 diverge. Continue beneath the river buttes and river bluffs along WI 60. About 5 miles out of Spring Green, a left onto Sauk County C starts a winding, 13-mile journey to Natural Bridge State Park. At the intersection with Sauk County Highway B, turn right to follow County C, and then turn left about 0.5 mile later. At the stop sign and junction with Sauk County Highway PF, turn right, and then left in the town of Leland. The park is another 1.5 miles down County C. Natural Bridge State Park is home to Wisconsin's largest natural bridge, a sandstone arch 25 feet high and 35 feet wide, carved by the combined effects of wind and water erosion, gravity, and frost. A rock shelter near the base of the arch has yielded artifacts dated at twelve thousand years old, making this one of the oldest known inhabited sites in the Midwest. The arch and shelter are found 0.25 mile down the trail leading from the parking lot.

Head back the way you came until you return to the intersection with County B. County C turns right, but you want to turn left and follow County B to WI 60. At WI 60, turn left and drive 5 miles to Sauk City, the end of this drive. The Sauk Prairie Area Chamber of Commerce distributes maps and directions for self-guided auto tours of the town's distinctive "block and stack" architecture, favored by the German and Swiss immigrants who settled here.

18

The Lead Region
A History Lesson: Stumbling Toward Statehood

General description: This drive loops through the southwest corner of the state, touring the first area of Wisconsin to be heavily settled by Europeans. Brought by the discovery of lead in 1827, miners, land speculators, and merchants flooded into the lead-rich area around Mineral Point. The drive passes a plethora of mines, as well as the site of Wisconsin's first capitol and the Swiss settlement in New Glarus. Today, dairy cows dot the steep hills around New Glarus and Yellowstone Lake State Park, and from Platteville to Monroe immense fields of corn stand on the rolling prairie.
Special attractions: Swiss Village Museum, Yellowstone Lake State Park, Pendarvis State Historical Site, First Capitol State Park, the Bevans Mine, the Badger Mine, Browntown-Cadiz Springs State Recreational Area, New Glarus Woods State Park, history, camping, hiking, biking, camping, fishing.
Location: The southwestern corner of Wisconsin. The drive starts and ends in New Glarus.
Drive route numbers: Wisconsin Highways 11, 23, 39, 69, 78, and 80, U.S. Highway 151, Lafayette County Highways F and G.
Travel season: Year-round.
Camping: 129 sites at Yellowstone Lake State Park, 18 drive-in and 14 hike-in sites at New Glarus Woods State Park.
Services: Full services in Monroe and Platteville.

 The drive

This drive starts in New Glarus, 25 miles southwest of Madison at the intersection of Wisconsin Highways 39 and 69. Hard times hit Glarus, Switzerland, in the 1840s, and on April 16, 1845, nearly two hundred citizens of Glarus left their homes for America. The group sent scouts ahead to find a place to plant New Glarus. The scouts traveled through Eastern and Midwestern states, and after finding the Little Sugar River valley to be an excellent place to raise dairy cows and generally recreate the pastoral bliss of their homeland, they sent for the rest of the group. On August 15, 1845, 108 members of the original party arrived in New Glarus. Each of the thirteen buildings at the Swiss Village Museum, on Sixth Street, represents a different facet of everyday life in the nineteenth-century Midwest: a newspaper office, settler's cabin, blacksmith shop, cheese factory, school house, and general store. Around town you'll find Swiss architecture, Swiss cheese, chocolate, pastries—and, if you listen closely, you might hear some of the Swiss-German dialect still spoken here.

Head west on WI 39. After approximately 10 miles, turn left onto Wisconsin Highway 78. In Blanchardville, turn right onto Lafayette County Highway F and travel approximately 5 miles to North Lake Road. Turn left and follow the winding, hilly road to Yellowstone Lake State Park. Lamenting the lack of large lakes in southwestern Wisconsin, the Department of Natural Resources dammed the Yellowstone River in 1954, creating 450-acre Yellowstone Lake. The western end of the lake is a waterfowl refuge, home to wood ducks and mallards in the summer, and a stopping point for loons, herons, bald eagles, osprey, and Canada geese in the spring and fall migrations. The park has 129 campsites, a beach, 7 miles of hiking trails, and 3 miles of biking trails. At the intersection with Lake Road, turn right and follow Lake Road along the lake and through the park. Where Lake Road intersects with County F, turn left.

Approximately 2 miles down County F, turn right onto Lafayette County G and follow County G west 7 miles to Wisconsin Highway 23. Turn right and travel north 7 miles to Mineral Point. The discovery of surface lead in the hills around Mineral Point in 1827 set off Wisconsin's lead rush and brought the first big wave of European settlement into the state. Wisconsin's European population quickly boomed from a very few to more than twenty thousand. Seven years after the start of the lead rush, the United States Congress created the Territory of Wisconsin. Colonel Henry Dodge, a veteran of the War of 1812 and the Black Hawk War, and a leader of the U.S. Dragoons, was sworn in as Governor at Mineral Point on July 4, 1836. Since housing was in short supply in mining boom towns like Mineral Point, many a miner lived in a house dug into the side of a hill, and thus Wisconsin picked up the nickname of the Badger State. Most of the easily accessible lead deposits were played out by 1848, and news of the discovery of gold in California that same year lured Wisconsin miners westward. By the 1870s, zinc mining had surpassed lead mining as the chief local industry. Zinc mining reached its peak in 1917 and then declined steadily until the last area mine closed in 1979.

In the 1830s, skilled hard-rock miners from Cornwall, England, left their exhausted tin mines and made for Mineral Point to seek their fortunes in lead. The Pendarvis State Historical Site preserves several of the Cornish miners' cottages on Shake Rag Street, so named because the miners' wives would shake a white rag out the window to call the men home from the mines for lunch. Costumed guides lead walking tours through the complex

Drive 18: The Lead Region
A History Lesson: Stumbling toward Statehood

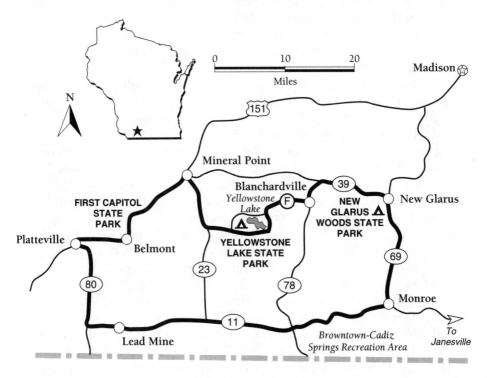

of limestone cottages filled with artifacts from the days of the Cornish miners.

Take U.S. Highway 151 south from Mineral Point 13 miles to Belmont. In Belmont, turn right onto Lafayette County Highway G and travel to First Capital State Park, which marks the site of Wisconsin's first Territorial Legislature meeting held in October through December of 1836. One of the primary pieces of business for the session was the selection of the site of the territory's permanent capital. The legislature was made up of land speculators, bankers, and others with monetary interests based in their various localities, and the fight to be home to the capitol was intense. The U.S. Congress had appropriated $20,000 to fund construction of government buildings, and delegates would be sure to get some of that money if their site were chosen.

Though he was not a delegate to the congress, land speculator James

Doty arrived in Belmont on November 2, 1836. Upon arrival, Doty began handing out buffalo robes to the delegates, who were crowded into a drafty, ill-heated building at the onset of winter. Doty then managed to sell or give away lots from his 1,360-acre Four Lakes property to 16 legislators, the clerks of both houses of the legislature, a Supreme Court Justice, and the Governor's son. When the votes were tallied, Doty's Four Lakes property (a.k.a. Madison) had been selected as the permanent home of the government. The park today features two of the buildings (one served time as a barn after the congress) used by the delegates, with exhibits, artifacts, and a diorama on the Belmont Legislative Session.

Head back to Belmont on County G, and then turn right on US 151 and travel west to Platteville. The Platteville Mining Museum traces the development of lead and zinc mining in the area. Guided tours descend into the Bevans Mine, which produced more than two million pounds of lead ore in 1845. A train takes visitors around the museum grounds in ore cars pulled by a 1931 mine locomotive. The adjacent Rollo Jamison Museum is the creation of life-long collector Rollo Jamison and houses his collection of more than twenty thousand local historical artifacts, including arrowheads, art, tools, and games from the early 1900s. The Chicago Bears football team holds its pre-season training at the University of Wisconsin, Platteville from mid-July to mid-August each year; practice schedules can be obtained from the Platteville Chamber of Commerce.

Head south on Wisconsin Highway 80 from Platteville. Approximately 11 miles from Platteville, turn left on Wisconsin Highway 11. In Benton, Swindler's Ridge Museum displays military and mining artifacts and maintains the 1851 village schoolhouse. In Shullsburg, 8 miles east of Benton, you can tour the Badger Mine and Museum. The Badger Mine was hand-dug in 1827, and the main passage is a half-mile long. The museum also recreates the nineteenth century mining town in an exhibit of shops and mining tools and artifacts. Continue east 25 miles through the town of Browntown to the Browntown-Cadiz Springs Recreational Area. To get to the 600-acre, day-use only (no camping) area, which offers two lakes, a beach, hiking trails, and a picnic area, turn right onto South Cadiz-Springs Road.

Monroe, 8 miles east of Browntown, calls itself the "Swiss Cheese Capital of the World." The town's first European settlers were Swiss who came here from the New Glarus area. The city boasts the only Limburger cheese factory in the country, and three of the area's largest employers are cheese factories. The Monroe Area Chamber of Commerce publishes a walking tour map of historic buildings in town, such as the Green County Courthouse, the 1857 Idle Hour Mansion, and the Green County Historical Museum, housed in a church built in 1861. The Cheese Country Recreational Trail is a 47-mile, multiple-use trail running on abandoned railroad grade along the

Early Cornish miners' homes in Mineral Point. Wisconsin Department of Tourism photo

Pecatonica River from Monroe to Mineral Point. Hikers, bikers, equestrians, and all-terrain vehicle riders use the trail in the summer months, and snowmobilers and cross-country skiers run the trail in the winter.

Travel north 15 miles on WI 69 from Monroe to New Glarus Woods State Park, 350 acres of forest, prairie, and farmland. Nearly 8 miles of hiking and biking trails meander through oak, elm, basswood, and black walnut trees in this hardwood forest. The family campground has eighteen drive-in sites, and fourteen primitive, hike-in sites are scattered throughout the park.

19

Janesville to Baraboo
Clowns, Trolls, and Terminal Moraines

General description: This 115-mile drive follows the curving line of hills from Janesville to Baraboo that marks the final extent of the last Ice Age glacier. This border land between the glaciated southeastern part of the state and the unglaciated southwestern part of the state is home to effigy mounds, trolls, Norwegians, and Devil's Lake. Baraboo is the northern terminus of the drive and the birthplace of the Ringling Brothers Circus—the circus performs daily during the summer at the Circus World Museum.

Special attractions: Ice Age Trail, Blue Mound State Park, Devil's Lake State Park, Cave of the Mounds, Little Norway, Wollersheim Winery, camping, hiking, biking, wildlife watching.

Location: Southern Wisconsin, near Madison.

Drive route numbers: U.S. Highways 14 and 18/151, Wisconsin Highways 92, 78, 60, 188 113 and 123, Dane County Highway ID, Sauk County Highway DL.

Travel season: Year-round.

Camping: 78 sites at Blue Mound State Park, 415 sites at Devil's Lake State Park.

Services: Full services in Janesville, Mount Horeb, and Baraboo.

 The drive

When the last glacier came scraping through Wisconsin, ten to twenty-five thousand years ago, it missed the southwestern part of the state. The glacier did not advance as a unified body, but had many sections, called lobes, that advanced and retreated at a pace somewhat independent of each other. This drive follows the terminal moraine—the line of hills left at the farthest extent of the glacier's Green Bay lobe. When the glacier began to melt and retreat, it dropped the rock and debris it had carried and pushed along its advancing edge. On the west side of the terminal moraine is the Driftless Area, the part of southern Wisconsin that escaped the glacial bulldozer. The terminal moraine here is a collection of dry, narrow ridges sitting

Drive 19: Janesville to Baraboo
Clowns, Trolls, and Terminal Moraines

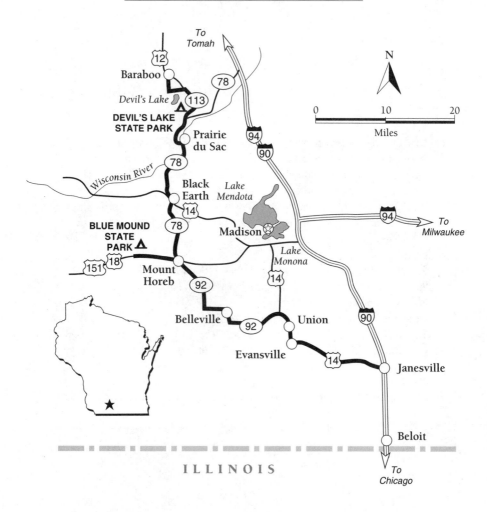

atop the older hills at the edge of the Driftless Area. The combination of glacial hills and the rolling, deeply-cut upland of the Driftless Area make for an area of varied landscape and beauty.

Janesville is home to roughly twenty percent of all Wisconsin buildings listed on the National Register of Historic Places, boasting ten historic districts with a variety of both commercial and residential architectural styles. Maps and information on historic district tours can be obtained at the Janesville Chamber of Commerce. The Rock County Historical Museum's extensive collection of local pictures and artifacts is an excellent complement to a tour of its architectural history. The Ice Age Trail (the 1,000-mile hiking trail that follows the glacier's moraines across the state) runs through Janesville using the city's system of parks and greenways.

Take U.S. Highway 14 west 18 miles to Evansville. Follow US 14 where it turns right in Evansville, and travel through Union. Approximately 3 miles out of Union, turn left onto Wisconsin Highway 92. Continue through Brooklyn, and you'll soon come to a wetland restoration/wildlife viewing area, where you're likely to see deer, waterfowl, songbirds, and other wetland critters. In Dayton, the road crosses the Sugar River. Approximately 4 miles from Dayton, watch the signs to follow where WI 92 takes first a right, then a left, into Belleville. Beyond Belleville, WI 92 runs in the valley of a branch of the Sugar River, and the road winds past farms snuggled low into the protected valley.

Trolls are everywhere in Mount Horeb, on signs, lawns, and street banners. It's a Norwegian thing. In fact, you'll find Little Norway (as well as Blue Mound State Park and Cave of the Mounds) west of Mount Horeb off U.S. Highway 18/151. A left onto US 18/151 at the first stop light in Mount Horeb takes you through the troll-happy town. Continue on US 18/151 out of Mount Horeb (you are now west of the terminal moraine and traveling through the Driftless Area), and exit at Cave of the Mounds Road approxi-

Devil's Lake.

mately 5 miles from town. Turn right on Dane County Highway ID and travel 0.25 mile to Little Norway, a farmstead settled by Norwegians in 1856. The farmstead evokes Norwegian-American history with log buildings, an 1893 wooden church, and, for the music buffs out there, an 1873 manuscript penned by Norwegian composer Edvard Grieg. Cave of the Mounds, a National Natural Landmark found west of Little Norway on County ID, is famous for the color, diversity, and delicacy of its chambers, tunnels, stalagmites, and stalactites. The cave remains a cool 50 degrees year-round, so have a sweater handy.

Continue on County ID to the town of Blue Mound and follow the signs to Blue Mound State Park. The highest point in these parts, Blue Mound has been a southwestern Wisconsin landmark for centuries. The flat-topped mound rises sharply from the land below, and the park's two observation towers offer amazing vistas of the surrounding Driftless Area hills, valleys, and farms. Blue Mound was once a relay point for National Weather Service weather data transmitted east from Pike's Peak, Colorado, to Lapham Peak, Wisconsin (Drive 1); the information was used to warn Great Lakes ports of impending storms. The park has 78 campsites, 11 miles of hiking trails, and 5 miles of biking trails.

Head back to Mount Horeb on US 18/151. At the WI 92 and US 18/151 intersection in Mount Horeb, turn left onto Wisconsin Highway 78 from US 18/151. If you skipped the side trip to Little Norway and Blue Mound, go forward at the WI 92 US 18/151 intersection—WI 92 ends at the intersection, and the road that continues north is WI 78. For the 10 miles between Mount Horeb and Black Earth, the road runs between hills dotted with dairy cows. In Black Earth, turn left where WI 78 joins US 14. Two miles out of town, turn right and follow WI 78 where the roads diverge. About 5 miles from that last intersection, the road runs above the Wisconsin River.

At the intersection with Wisconsin Highway 60, you have options. The main route turns left here and crosses the river into Prairie du Sac. For a quick side trip to the historic Wollersheim Winery, turn right onto WI 60 and then left onto Wisconsin Highway 188. First planted as a vineyard in the 1840s by Hungarian Count Agostan Haraszthy, the property was purchased by the Kehl family when the Count left town to seek a new fortune in the California Gold Rush. Haraszthy later became known as the founder of the California wine industry, and the vineyards he started here are still producing under the Wollersheim Winery name. The limestone winery's architecture features arched wine cellars, a carriage house, and a grand hall with a dance floor.

After crossing the Wisconsin River into Prairie du Sac, turn right and follow WI 78 north, and then turn left onto Wisconsin Highway 113 after approximately 8 miles and travel to Devil's Lake State Park. To find Devil's Lake (the body of water), turn left onto Sauk County Highway DL and then left again at the sign to the park office. Devil's Lake occupies a section of an ancient river valley called the Devil's Lake Gap that was blocked on both ends by the glacial debris of the Green Bay lobe's terminal moraine. The spring-fed lake today varies in depth from 40 to 50 feet, and the surrounding bluffs rise 500 feet from the shoreline.

Devil's Lake State Park is one of the nine units of the Ice Age National Scientific Reserve, which was established in 1971 to protect and preserve the geological heritage of the Wisconsin glaciation. More than 20 miles of hiking trails wander all over the bluffs, passing such geological features as Balanced Rock and Devil's Doorway. The park also protects the landscaping created by a group of woodland Indians called the Effigy Mound Builders, who lived here about 1000 A.D. Three animal mounds (one resembling a lynx, one a bear, and one a bird) are still in good shape-the easiest to find is the lynx near the nature center. The 415-site campground was full when I visited in July, so don't be afraid to reserve a campsite ahead of time if you'd like to camp here.

When you're ready to move on from Devil's Lake, continue west on County DL, and then turn right onto Wisconsin Highway 123 to head for Baraboo, birthplace of the Ringling Brothers Circus. Sons of a German im-

View from south observation tower, Blue Mound State Park.

Panfrey's Glen, Devil's Lake State Park. WISCONSIN DEPARTMENT OF TOURISM PHOTO

migrant harness maker who had moved his family all over the Midwest (eventually settling in Baraboo), the five Ringling brothers vowed early in life that they would one day own a circus. They gave their first performance as the "Old Yankee Robinson and Ringling Bros. Double Show" in Baraboo on May 19, 1884. The brothers then took the show on the road in their colorful wagons, and later in trains, as they toured the continent from Maine to British Columbia. In 1891, the Ringling Brothers Circus grew from a one-ring to a three-ring show, and in 1907 the brothers purchased the Barnum & Bailey Circus. The circus had its winter quarters in Baraboo along the Baraboo River from 1884 to 1918 and supported hundreds of local craftsmen including wagon makers, carpenters, painters, blacksmiths, and seamstresses.

The Circus World Museum, on Water Street, sits on the site of what was the Ringling Brothers Circus winter quarters. The museum displays old-time circus memorabilia year-round, and in the summer offers daily circus events including live circus performances under a 2,000-seat Big Top. On Fourth Street, the Al Ringling Theater (completed in 1915 at a cost of $100,000) offers tours through the plush performance hall. A few of the brothers built large homes in town, but none could outshine circus leader Al Ringling's mansion built in 1905 and located at the corner of Broadway and Fifth streets. Other historic circus sites are scattered around town—you can't miss them.

That concludes this drive. From here, you can head south to Sauk City for Drive 17, or head east to Portage for Drive 20, which will take you past the mega-attraction called Wisconsin Dells.

20

Wisconsin Dells

Failed Canals and Ancient Lakeshores

General description: This 95-mile drive follows U.S. Highway 12 as it runs along the border between the flat lands to the east (the bed of what was once a huge lake) and the hilly lands of the Dirftless Area to the west. Starting in Portage, the route goes through Wisconsin Dells, detours to a cottage designed by Frank Lloyd Wright, and then heads northwest past rugged bluffs and through the Black River State Forest, camping, hiking.

Special attractions: Portage Canal, Wisconsin Dells, Mirror Lake State Park, Rocky Arbor State Park, Wisconsin National Guard Museum, Mill Bluff State Park, Black River State Forest, camping, hiking.

Location: Southcentral to western Wisconsin, starting in Portage and ending in Black River Falls.

Drive route numbers: Wisconsin Highway 16, U.S. Highway 12.

Travel season: Year-round.

Camping: 144 sites at Mirror Lake State Park, 89 sites at Rocky Arbor State Park, 21 sites at Mill Bluff State Park, and 38 and 37 sites at the Pigeon Creek and Castle Mound campgrounds, respectively, in the Black River State Forest.

Services: Full services in Portage, Wisconsin Dells, Tomah, and Black River Falls.

 The drive

This drive begins in Portage, where for hundreds of years river travelers portaged (carried) their canoes and supplies across the 1.5 miles of swamp between the Fox and Wisconsin Rivers. The portage links the St. Lawrence Seaway and the Mississippi watershed, and was already a trade center inhabited by the Winnebagos when the French arrived in 1673. The French explorers Marquette and Joliet were the first Europeans to use the portage here, and they were soon followed by legions of French *voyageurs* and fur traders.

The Winnebagos officially ceded the land here to the U.S. government in the Treaty of 1828. In the same year, Congress directed that Fort Winnebago be built here to protect this important trade and military route.

Fort Winnebago was the third of three forts (with Fort Howard at the mouth of the Fox River at Green Bay and Fort Crawford at the confluence of the Wisconsin and Mississippi Rivers at Prairie du Chien) on what was once Wisconsin's most important water highway. Two structures remain today at the site of Fort Winnebago. The first is the Indian Agency House, built by the U.S. government in 1832 for its Indian agent to the local Winnebagos, and it has been restored and furnished with antiques of that era. The second is the Surgeon's Quarters, a house built between 1819 and 1828 by Francois LeRoi, who operated a business portaging goods between the rivers. You can find both buildings on Wisconsin Highway 33 on the east side of town.

Hoping to improve the trade route between the St. Lawrence and Mississippi watersheds, local residents planned a canal connecting the Upper Fox and Lower Wisconsin Rivers. Digging began in 1838, but it wasn't until 1876 that the Army Corps of Engineers completed the 2.5-mile canal and opened it to navigation. In 1886, the feds gave up maintenance of the Wisconsin River section of the canal because shifting sandbars and erratic water levels often blocked passage for larger boats. Smaller pleasure crafts continued to use the canal until 1961, when the Wisconsin River locks were welded shut and the Fort Winnebago locks were replaced by an earthen dam. Part of the canal has been restored, and you can walk along a section of the canal as it runs through town.

Head west on Wisconsin Highway 16 and travel 11 miles along the Wisconsin River to Wisconsin Dells, the state's largest tourist attraction. There is no denying the beauty of the sandstone palisades, narrow gorges, high cliffs, rocky island, canyons and sculpted sandstone formations on the Wisconsin River that first attracted settlers and vacationers. Ancient sandstone deposits that went untouched by glaciers have instead been deeply cut by thousands of years of erosion. Quite a number of river-tour outfits will take you through the formations in both the Upper and Lower Dells. If you're in the mood for other distractions, Wisconsin Dells is brimming with them: water slides, mini-golf, go-carts, waterski shows, and a plethora of other entertainment options await.

Continue through Wisconsin Dells, on WI 16/U.S. Highway 12, or, for a quick side trip to Mirror Lake State Park and a cottage designed by Frank Lloyd Wright, take US 12 east approximately 8 miles and follow the signs to Mirror Lake State Park. The lake itself was created when Horace LaBar dammed Dell Creek in the mid-nineteenth century to power his flour mill. The mill continued to operate under various owners until 1957, when it burned to the ground. The state acquired the property in 1961 and established Mirror Lake State Park. The Seth Peterson Cottage sits balanced on the edge of a wooded sandstone bluff overlooking Mirror Lake. Peterson convinced the aging Wright to design a cottage for him in 1958, but Peterson never did live in it—he died before it was completed. The cottage fell into

Drive 20: Wisconsin Dells
Failed Canals and Ancient Lakeshores

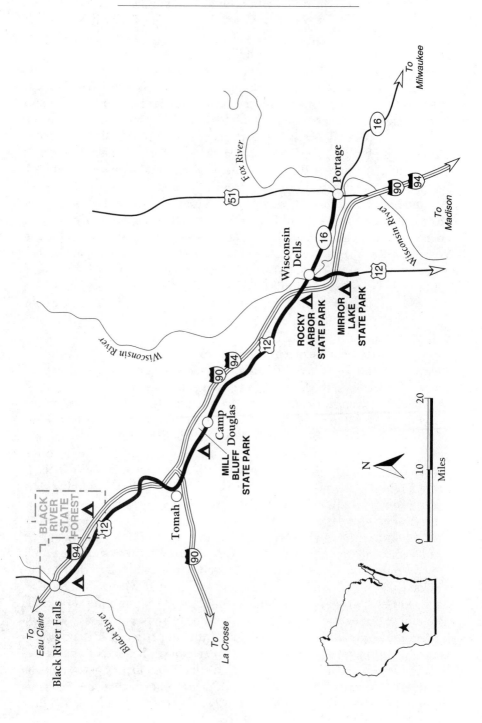

Bluffs at Mill Bluff State Park.

disrepair, and the State picked up the building and surrounding property in 1966 in an expansion of the state park. The cottage, with its flagstone floors, sandstone walls, and massive fireplace, can be rented year round and is open to public tours on the second Sunday of each month from 1 to 4 P.M. Mirror Lake State Park has 144 campsites, a beach, a picnic area, a boat launch, and hiking and cross-country skiing trails.

Take US 12 west from either Mirror Lake State Park or Wisconsin Dells to Rocky Arbor State Park, 1 mile west of Wisconsin Dells. Established in 1932, the 230-acre state park protects a sandstone gorge cut by the Wisconsin River thousands of years ago (the river has since changed course and now flows about 1.5 miles east of the park). A nature trail wanders all over the gorge, passing many beautiful sandstone formations. The park's 89-site campground has showers, flush toilets, and electricity.

As you continue west on US 12 through the towns of Lyndon Station, Mauston, and New Lisbon, you're running along the edge of what was once Glacial Lake Wisconsin. On the left side of the road is the Driftless Area, the hilly southwestern corner of Wisconsin that was untouched by glaciers. On the right side of the road, the land is generally low, flat, and sandy, as it was once the bed of the huge lake that formed when glacial debris blocked the Wisconsin River near Wisconsin Dells. As the glacier melted, the backed-up meltwater became a very large spring puddle—Glacial Lake Wisconsin. It stretched from Wisconsin Dells north to Black River Falls, and east to Stevens Point. This borderland is a place of abrupt hills and high bluffs, as well as lakes and wetlands.

As you approach Camp Douglas, you will notice bluffs on both sides of the road. Prior to the formation of Glacial Lake Wisconsin, these bluffs were Driftless Area sandstone hills, like those you can see to the west. As the lake rose higher and higher, these hills became islands, and were subjected to erosion by the lake's waves crashing against them. When the Wisconsin River had cut a new course through the blockage near Wisconsin Dells, the lake drained and left the rugged, jutting hills which rise from the flat plain of the glacial lake bed to the east.

The village of Camp Douglas is home to the Wisconsin National Guard Museum, with 3,000 square feet of exhibits on the history of Wisconsin soldiers at war: from the Spanish-American War, through both World Wars, to the Gulf War. The grounds outside the museum feature tanks from yesteryear to today, plus howitzers and field guns. The airfield at the museum features historic and present-day military aircraft.

Mill Bluff State Park is found 2 miles beyond Camp Douglas on US 12, and is one of Wisconsin's nine Ice Age Scientific Reserve Units, which were established to protect and preserve the state's glacial heritage. Mill Bluff, which got its name from a sawmill here in the early days of settlement, is the highest bluff in the area, rising to an elevation of 1,123.5 feet above sea

Boat tours of the Wisconsin Dells are available. Wisconsin Department of Tourism photo

level. Several hiking trails (some more difficult than others) lead from the south parking lot over and around Mill Bluff, and two overlooks provide great vistas from the top of the bluff. The park has a beach, twenty-one campsites, and a picnic area.

Continue on US 12 to Tomah, named for a Menominee Indian chief who once gathered his tribe in this area for a conference. When you get into Tomah and turn right at the light to follow US 12, you're on Superior Avenue, also known as "Gasoline Alley" in honor of the comic strip of the same name created by Tomah native Frank King. At its height in the middle of the century, *Gasoline Alley* appeared in more than three hundred daily newspapers with a total circulation of more than twenty-five million. Place names for the strip, such as Fieting's Store, Humboldt Hill, and the Ridge, were frequently taken from Tomah. In 1959, the National Cartoon Society named King "Cartoonist of the Year" and *Gasoline Alley* the best strip of the year.

Approximately 13 miles out of Tomah, you cross through the southern part of the 66,000-acre Black River State Forest, established in 1857. The forest has an abundance of hiking, biking, horse-riding, cross-country skiing, snowmobiling and ATV trails, canoeing, camping, and picnic areas. Roughly ten thousand cords of wood products from the Black River State

Forest provide nearly $150,000 in state revenue each year. The Pigeon Creek Campground east of Millston has thirty-eight campsites—to find it, turn right onto Jackson County Highway O in Millston, then left onto the town road a quarter mile past the I-94 underpass, then right onto North Settlement Road and travel 1 mile to the campground. Beyond Millston, the route leaves the Black River State Forest and travels through the Jackson County Forest. About 8 miles out of Millston, you enter another section of the Black River State Forest. The Castle Mound Campground is found in this section, with thirty-seven campsites, hiking and cross-country skiing trails, a picnic area, and toilets.

The drive ends 1 mile past the campground in the town of Black River Falls, which began to grow as a logging town. The area's first sawmill opened in 1839, and at the height of the logging era, fifty sawmills were turning logs into lumber in Jackson County. The river where US 12 crosses in the middle of town is very rocky and scenic.

From Black River Falls you have several options. You can continue on US 12 for Drive 14 to Willow River State Park, or you can follow Wisconsin Highway 54 west through the Driftless Area for Drive 17, or you can follow WI 54 east through cranberry country to Waupaca for Drive 22.

21

Necedah National Wildlife Refuge
Refuges and Roche A Cri

General description: This drive rolls through the flat, sandy center part of the state that was once the bed of a huge glacial lake and travels Wisconsin Highway 173, the straightest road in Wisconsin, on the first leg of the drive. Among the featured stops are the Necedah National Wildlife Refuge, where you can see just about every sort of migratory bird that travels through the state, and Roche A Cri State Park, home to Roche A Cri, a 300-foot-high stack of sandstone that towers over the surrounding marshes.

Special attractions: Necedah National Wildlife Refuge, Meadow Valley Wildlife Area, Roche A Cri State Park, camping, hiking, biking, fishing, wildlife watching.

Location: Central Wisconsin, starting and ending just north of Tomah.

Drive route numbers: Wisconsin Highways 21, 173, and 13, Wood County Highway Z.

Travel season: Year-round.

Camping: 41 sites at Roche A Cri State Park.

Services: Full services in Tomah, south of the drive; limited services in Necedah and Nekoosa.

 The drive

This drive starts at the East Wisconsin Highway 21 exit from Interstate Highway 94 north of Tomah. Travel 5 miles east from I-94 on WI 21 to the junction with Wisconsin Highway 173 and turn left. Approximately 2 miles north on WI 173, you enter the Meadow Valley Wildlife Area. The white and red pines that originally dominated the forest here were logged off in the mid-1800s. Farmers dug numerous ditches in an attempt to drain the land and create cropland around the turn of the century, but the soil here is sandy and the growing season unpredictable. After falling into tax delinquency, most of the farms were abandoned. The federal government purchased the land, and the 90-square-mile Meadow Valley Wildlife Area was leased to the state of Wisconsin in 1940. Today it is administered under a cooperative agreement with the U.S. Fish and Wildlife Service, which also

Drive 21: Necedah National Wildlife Refuge
Refuges and Roche A Cri

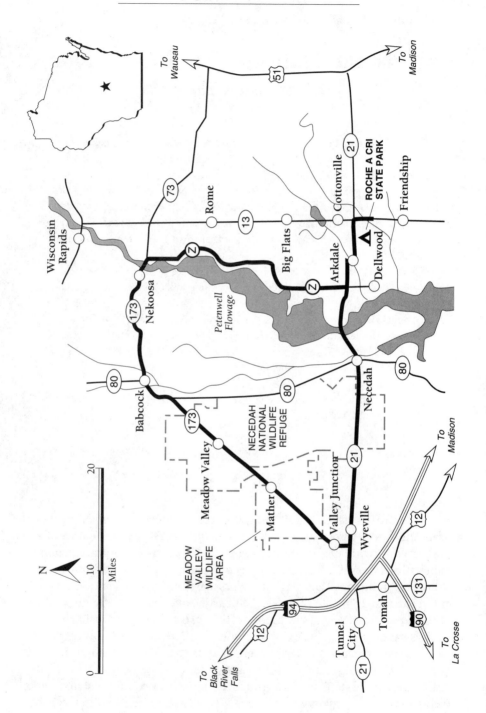

manages the Necedah National Wildlife Refuge to the east.

The land here was once the bed of a huge glacial lake called Glacial Lake Wisconsin, which formed at the end of the Ice Age (around eleven thousand years ago). At that time, the great glaciers were quickly melting. Far south of here, near Wisconsin Dells, the glacier dropped a huge pile of rock and gravel into the Wisconsin River Valley, blocking the principal drainage for the glacial runoff. The raging meltwaters were backed up, creating a huge lake over south-central Wisconsin. The land here is flat, with large marshes and low sandy ridges.

WI 173 is the straightest road in Wisconsin, rivaling the roads of western Kansas, where you can be in one prairie town and see the grain elevators of the town 15 miles behind, and the grain elevators of the town in the hazy heat 15 miles ahead of you. This is an area of mixed forests, with scattered meadows and open fields, tall grasses, deer, and birds. You'll also notice cranberry bogs in this area. Cranberries are grown commercially in five states: Massachusetts, New Jersey, Oregon, Washington, and Wisconsin. Wisconsin annually produces nearly one-third of the national cranberry crop. While cranberry marshes cover more than 110,000 acres of Wisconsin's land, the cranberries themselves are grown on less than one tenth of that acreage. The other 90 percent is support land, reservoirs, ditches, dikes, water control systems, wild uplands, and wetlands. Cranberry growing is generally an environmentally friendly venture—the plants are perrenials, and an established bed may be in production for more than one hundred years. As there is no plowing, cranberry farming doesn't erode the soil like other forms of farming, and the bogs act as wetlands, providing flood control, filtering particles from the water, slowing the discharge of heavy rains, and replenishing the aquifer, just as natural wetlands do.

Continue northeast on WI 173 through the town of Mather, 8 miles beyond Valley Junction, and Meadow Valley, 8 miles past Mather. Just beyond Mather, you enter the Necedah National Wildlife Refuge. *Necedah* is a Winnebago word meaning "land of yellow water." Water in the refuge is often yellowish due to high levels of iron (a few miles north of here, on Drive 22, Wazee Lake County Park sits on a reclaimed iron mine). Wetlands in the refuge have been restored since about 1940, mostly for migratory bird habitat. The ditches and dikes that were once used to drain the land are used today to manipulate water levels and provide optimal feeding, nesting, and resting areas for the birds. You're passing through the northwest corner of the refuge here—WI 21 on the last leg of the drive offers better access to the refuge.

At the intersection with Wisconsin Highway 80, turn left and follow WI 173/WI 80 for approximately 3 miles, and then turn right to follow WI 173 near the town of Babcock. Follow WI 173 for another 12 miles to Nekoosa (a Winnebago word meaning "running waters"). In the mid-1880s,

Petenwell Lake.

Nekoosa was a settlement called Point Basse, begun by Robert Wakely, who, besides ferrying travelers across the river, ran an inn and post office. Wakely's outpost, located at the end of a long set of rapids on the Wisconsin River, became a major stopping point for lumber rafts headed down river. The first sawmill in the area was built in Nekoosa in 1831, and the town today is still closely tied to the timber industry.

Travel through Nekoosa on WI 173 and cross the Wisconsin River-notice the bluffs at the river crossing. Just after you cross the river, turn right onto Wood County Highway Z. County Z follows the eastern shore of the 23,000-acre Petenwell Flowage of the Wisconsin River (the state's second largest inland body of water), which was created when the river was dammed to the south just above the WI 21 bridge across the Wisconsin River. There are various beaches and trails along the water's edge on this stretch. Approximately 20 miles south of WI 173, you'll find the Petenwell County Park, which sits on a point sticking out into the flowage. The park has a swimming beach, hiking and biking trails, and plenty of good fishing.

Continue south on County Z for 5 miles to the junction with WI 21, turn left, and travel approximately 7 miles to Wisconsin Highway 13. Turn right onto WI 13 and travel 2 miles to 450-acre Roche A Cri State Park. *Roche A Cri* is the name the French fur traders gave to the 300-foot-high sandstone outcropping of rock that rises abruptly from the surrounding

Canada geese on their migration south. WISCONSIN DEPARTMENT OF TOURISM PHOTO

marshes. You'll find a spectacular view of the surrounding countryside from the end of the staircase leading to the top of the rock. The park's wooded campground has forty-one sites, and if the walk to the top of Roche A Cri wasn't enough exercise, you can hike some of the park's 4.2 miles of trails.

Head back to WI 21, turn left, and travel west. Where WI 21 crosses the Wisconsin River, about 10 miles from WI 13, you'll find a great picnic spot on the east bank of the river. The river here has cut a deep channel through the rock, leaving high bluffs on both sides. Cross the river and travel through Necedah. A couple of miles west of Necedah, you're back at the Necedah National Wildlife Refuge. A right turn on Headquarters Road will take you to refuge headquarters, which is close to two great wildlife watching spots—a wetland observation deck and The Rynerson Wetlands Observation Tower. Both are great spots to watch migratory birds in the spring and fall. You're likely to spot ducks, geese, eagles, osprey, and sandhill cranes. Head east down the trail that crosses the road shortly before the headquarters to get to the observation deck; a right turn at the headquarters and the intersection with Grand Dike Road will take you to the observation tower. The headquarters itself has oodles of information on the refuge and the wildlife found within and around its boundaries. The refuge has many miles of hiking and biking trails, but it is day use only, and no camping is allowed.

To finish the drive, continue west down WI 21 for 22 miles to I-94.

22

Wisconsin Highway 54
Cranberry Country

General description: This drive follows Wisconsin Highway 54 from Black River Falls to Hartman Creek State Park near Waupaca. Central Wisconsin's cranberry country is a wide, sandy wetland that was once the bed of a huge Ice Age lake called Glacial Lake Wisconsin. The route starts in the hills at Black River Falls, crosses the flat cranberry bogs, and then climbs up a line of hills left by the glacier twelve thousand years ago.

Special attractions: Black River State Forest, Jackson County Forest, Wazee Lake County Park, cranberry bogs, Hartman Creek State Park, scuba diving, camping, hiking, biking, cross-country skiing, fishing.

Location: Western and Central Wisconsin.

Drive route numbers: Wisconsin Highway 54.

Travel season: Year-round.

Camping: 37 sites at Castle Mound State Forest Campground, 12 sites at Wazee Lake County Park, 26 sites at East Fork State Forest Campground, 15 sites at Crawford Hills Campground, 25 sites at Spaulding Pond County Park, 56 sites at Hartman Creek State Park.

Services: Full services in Black River Falls and Wisconsin Rapids, limited elsewhere.

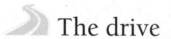 The drive

This drive starts in Black River Falls on the edge of the Black River State Forest. Black River Falls began as a logging town. The area's first sawmill opened in 1839, and at the height of the logging era, fifty sawmills were turning logs into lumber in Jackson County. The falls from which the town draws its name was dammed a long time ago to turn the blades of the sawmill, but where Wisconsin Highway 54 crosses the river in the middle of town, the river is rocky and lined by the white pines that initially brought lumberjacks to the area. The Castle Mound State Forest Campground is found 1 mile south of town on U.S. Highway 12 and has thirty-seven campsites, great hiking and cross-country skiing trails leading through wooded hills, a picnic area, and toilets.

Head east out of Black River Falls on WI 54, and you soon enter the Jackson County Forest. After a few miles, just past the casino, you'll see a sign for Wazee Lake County Park. The road to the park is a right turn, and just across from it you'll see a historical marker with a clearing behind it. If you're traveling this route on either Memorial Day or Labor Day, you'll see a Winnebago pow-wow going on, with colorfully-dressed dancers and spectators moving to music. The Winnebago, also known as the Ho-Chunk, inhabited central and southern Wisconsin when the first French fur traders arrived. As lumbering and farming brought more and more European settlers to the region, the Winnebago, like other Native American tribes in the southern half of the state, were resettled to the west. The Winnebago were forcibly relocated to Nebraska, but the treeless, lakeless prairie held little appeal for them.

So, a group of Winnebago led by Chief Winneshiek (the second of that name in recent history) returned to this area, and they still live here today. The historical marker commemorates the bravery of Mitchell Red Cloud, Jr., grandson of Winneshiek, who died while defending his fellow soldiers in the Korean War.

Follow the signs to Wazee Lake County Park (*wazee* means "tall pine" in the Winnebago language) for great views of the surrounding countryside. The park sits on a reclaimed iron mine, and in the center of the park there is still a huge pit from which the miners extracted the ore. The pit, fed by springs, has since filled with water, and the county claims that this is now the deepest, cleanest, and clearest lake (other than Lakes Superior and Michigan, of course) in the state. It is now popular with scuba divers.

The park is littered with huge chunks of granite, both piled up and strewn all about. The highest pile of mining till provides an excellent overlook of the lake and the land around it. From the top, you can see the hills of the Driftless Area (the southwestern part of Wisconsin untouched by the last Ice Age) to the west. In the foreground to the east are a few hills and bluffs, but beyond these hills the land is a flat, sandy, white pine- and cranberry-filled plain that was once the bed of a huge Ice Age lake called Glacial Lake Wisconsin. Far south of here, near Wisconsin Dells, the advancing glacier blocked the principal drainage for the state, the Wisconsin River Valley, with boulders and gravel. As the glacier melted, water backed up behind this natural dam and filled an area from Wisconsin Dells north to Black River Falls and east to just beyond Plover, a town due east of here on this drive. The park features twelve campsites, wildlife viewing, hiking, biking, fishing, swimming, and scuba diving.

Head back to WI 54, turn right onto WI 54 and drive east. You're now driving through the center of the 66,000-acre Black River State Forest. It is a working forest with more than one-fourth of its tree cover consisting of

Drive 22: Wisconsin Highway 54 Cranberry Country
Cranberry Country

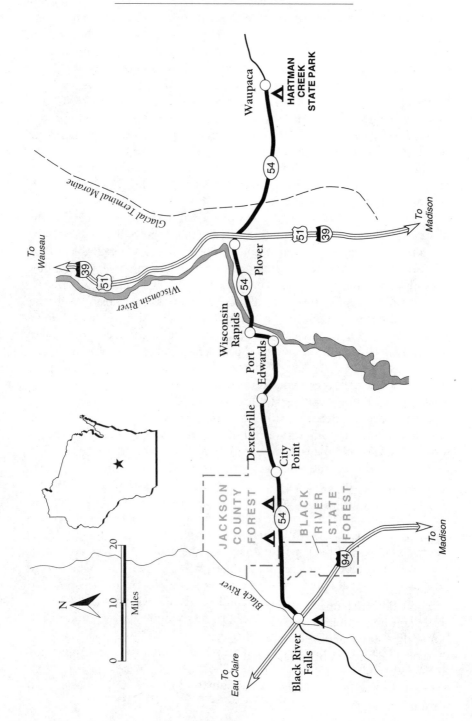

jack pine used in the local paper and pulp industries. There are also white pine and red pine plantations throughout the forest which are managed to provide sustained timber harvests, in contrast to the early logging industry, which cut down trees a forest at a time. Much of the labor for planting and brush clearing is supplied by the inmates of the Black River Correctional Facility (I suppose it could be worse—they could be breaking rocks). Backpacking is popular on the 24 miles of hiking trails, and there are numerous lakes, rivers, and streams, as well as sandstone ridges and isolated bluffs. There have been reports of the return of the Eastern timber wolf to the forest, so keep your eyes open and you might just see one. A left at the sign to the State Forest Campground will take you to the edge of the forest (about 6 miles north) and the East Fork Campground on the East Fork of the Black River, with twenty-six campsites, a picnic area, firewood, a playground, hiking trails, and a swimming beach.

Approximately 7 miles from the road to the state forest campground, you're out of the state forest and back into the Jackson County Forest, on the approach to the Crawford Hills County Park, with fifteen campsites, hiking trails, and a playground. Approximately 5 miles farther east, you'll find the Spaulding Pond County Park, with twenty-five campsites, fishing, hiking trails, and swimming. East of Spaulding Pond, you enter the flat, wetland plain left by Glacial Lake Wisconsin. Just beyond City Point, 28 miles from Black River Falls, you cross into Wood County and cranberry country. Early farmers in this area built dikes and drainages to remove the water and grow wheat. It was a doomed venture from the start, and they soon found that they couldn't fight the water and win. Cranberries grew wild in the area, and in the 1870s the first bogs were carved out of the wetland by hand. Today, several cranberry farms are located along WI 54 between City Point and Wisconsin Rapids. Cranberries are grown commercially in five states: Massachusets, New Jersey, Oregon, Washington, and Wisconsin. Wisconsin annually produces nearly one-third of the national cranberry crop. While cranberry marshes cover more than 110,000 acres of Wisconsin's land, the cranberries themselves are grown on less than 10 percent of that acreage. The other 90 percent is support land, reservoirs, ditches, dikes, water control systems, wild uplands, and wetlands.

In Dexterville, 13 miles east of City Point, WI 54 turns right after passing Lake Dexter, then left less than 1 mile later. Travel another 12 miles to Point Edwards, one of the many paper mill towns along the Wisconsin River and home to a Georgia Pacific mill that produces office paper. Turn left at the T-intersection and follow WI 54 along the Wisconsin River into Wisconsin Rapids. A historical marker on this stretch marks the birthplace of the Wisconsin paper industry, where Centralia Pulp & Water Company converted a saw mill into a pulp and paper mill in 1887. The mill operated until it burned to the ground in 1912. Turn right and cross the bridge over

Hartman Creek State Park.

the river in Wisconsin Rapids to follow WI 54. Wisconsin Rapids is still a paper mill town; the local economy is dominated by Consolidated Papers, makers of glossy paper for magazines and catalogs. On Third Street, the South Wood County Historical Museum (open Tuesdays, Thursdays, and Sundays, May through October) displays the area's cranberry history and recreates Wood County life of a century ago, with a general store, doctor's office, and other exhibits. If you've got kids along, you can let them run at the Wisconsin Rapids Municipal Zoo at 1900 Gaynor Avenue, which has native Wisconsin animals, a petting zoo, and a playground and picnic area. The zoo is open Memorial Day through Labor Day, closed Mondays.

Continue on WI 54 out of Wisconsin Rapids. For the 16 miles between Wisconsin Rapids and Plover, WI 54 is a four-lane highway occasionally lined by white pine. WI 54 turns right at a stoplight in Plover—follow the signs pointing to Waupaca. The route crosses over U.S. Highway 51/Interstate Highway 39, and you'll notice the land begin to change. The forests are hardwoods, not pines, and corn fields and dairy cows dot the gently rolling hills. Near the intersection with Portage County Highway J, the road climbs steeply. The hill you're driving up is actually the terminal moraine left by the last Ice Age glacier. The terminal moraine, which runs north-south here, is a long line of hills made up of the debris pushed and carried along the front edge of the glacier. When the glacier stopped its advance and began melting twelve thousand years ago, all the boulders, sand and gravel riding the front of the glacier were dropped; the terminal moraine clearly marks the farthest extent of the glacier across the state.

Approximately 17 miles out of Plover, turn right at the sign to Hartman Creek State Park and the end of this drive. Named for the creek that runs through it, Hartman Creek State Park contains a section of the Ice Age Trail (a 1,000 mile hiking trail that follows the moraines left by the last glacier) as well as 15 miles of other hiking trails, 56 campsites, biking trails, and a swimming beach. You can fish for bluegills and largemouth bass or paddle a canoe on any of the park's five lakes.

From here it's a short trip to the Wisconsin Veteran's Home in King, the start of Drive 4.

23

Wausau and Environs
Smack Dab in the Middle

General description: This drive wanders through the part of the state I know best, the rolling hills of central Wisconsin around Wausau. Starting at the waterfalls and rocky river trails of Dells of the Eau Claire County Park, the drive follows country roads through the rolling hills east, west, and north of Wausau, and ends at Council Grounds State Park north of Merrill. Along the way, you'll find the state's third-highest peak, fields of corn and ginseng, forests, streams, and all the cultural amenities of the Wausau area.

Special attractions: Dells of the Eau Claire County Park, Leigh Yawkey Woodson Art Museum, Marathon Park, Rib Mountain State Park, Council Grounds State Park, camping, fishing, swimming, hiking, biking, cross-country skiing.

Location: Smack dab in the middle of the state.

Drive route numbers: Wisconsin Highways 29, 64, and 107, Marathon County Highways Y, Z, J, and N.

Travel season: Year-round.

Camping: 25 sites at Dells of the Eau Claire County Park, 45 sites at Marathon Park, 30 sites at Rib Mountain State Park, 55 sites at Council Grounds State Park.

Services: Full services in Wausau and Merrill.

 The drive

This drive starts at the Dells of the Eau Claire County Park. To get there, take Wisconsin Highway 29 east from Wausau approximately 20 miles to Hatley, turn left onto Marathon County Highway Y, and travel north. At the intersection with Marathon County Highway N, roughly 6 miles from WI 29, go straight, and at the intersection with Marathon County Highway Z, turn left and follow County Y/County Z for about 1 mile. Turn right at the sign to the park and follow County Y across the Eau Claire River. After you cross the river, the campground is on your right, but continue up the hill and turn left into the park. Park in the lot and head down the trail back to the river, and you're at the Dells—a rocky, constricted section of the river

Dells of the Eau Claire River.

with several small waterfalls. On a hot summer day, there are few things finer than finding a quiet pool at the bottom of one of the falls and having a long soak. When you finish your soak, you can hike a section of the Ice Age Trail (the 1,000-mile hiking trail that follows the hills created by the last glacier 12,000 years ago), or try one of the trails along the river. The campground has 25 sites, and there is also a sandy beach, a playground, and a picnic area within the park.

Travel back down County Y to the intersection with County Z and turn right onto County Z. Travel approximately 8 miles on County Z to Marathon County Highway J, turn left onto County J. Follow County J until the intersection with Marathon County Highway N, turn right, and follow County N west into Wausau, originally known as Big Bull Falls. In 1850, Big Bull Falls had 15 operational sawmills and a population of 1,500 who decided to change the village's name to *Wausau*, meaning "far away" in the Ojibwe language. At the stop light and intersection with Business Highway 51, turn right and head north into downtown Wausau. Follow Business 51 approximately 1 mile to Stewart Avenue, turn left, and travel west through town. At 700 North Twelfth Street in Wausau, you'll find the Leigh Yawkey Woodson Art Museum in an English Cotswold-style mansion (open daily). The museum's permanent collection centers around bird art in painting,

Drive 23: Wausau and Environs
Smack Dab in the Middle

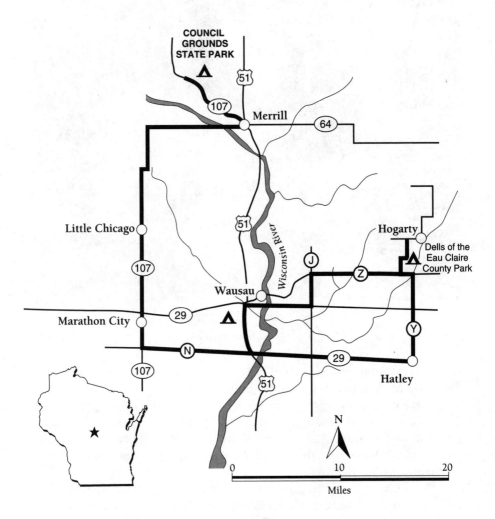

sculpture, and drawing. Rotating exhibits have featured works of Andy Warhol, paintings from the Russian Underground, and modern European pop prints. The Marathon County Historical Museum, at 403 McIndoe Street, is housed in a 1900 neo-classical home built for Cyrus Yawkey, one of Wausau's early prominent citizens. The museum recreates the Victorian era with an authentically-furnished music room, dining room, and parlor; the second and third floors feature rotating and visiting exhibits. After you cross the Wisconsin River on Stewart Avenue, you'll find Marathon County Park, home of the Wisconsin Valley Fair which takes place on the last weekend in July each year. The park also has forty-five campsites (most with electric hook-ups), showers, and hiking trails.

Continue west on Stewart Avenue to the intersection with U.S. Highway 51, turn south, and take US 51 to the Marathon County Highway N exit. Turn right at the bottom of the ramp, travel one block to the entrance to Rib Mountain State Park (long a landmark for both Native Americans and European settlers), and head up the hill. At 1,940 feet above sea level, Rib Mountain is the third-highest point in the state, and is mostly composed of unusually pure quartzite. At one point, Rib Mountain was barely a bump on the landscape. The area was the bottom of an inland sea before glaciers swept across the region. As the glaciers melted and the rushing meltwater streams eroded the softer sand and other material, only the hard quartzite remained, leaving the hill known as Rib Mountain. The mountain rises 650 feet above County N and 780 feet above Lake Wausau. Two observation decks and a 60-foot observation tower provide great views of the surrounding countryside. The two campgrounds at the park have a total of 40 campsites, and 7.5 miles of hiking trails will send you wandering all over the quartzite wonder. Head back down the mountain and turn right onto County N. As you travel west, you're rolling along south of the long axis of Rib Mountain. A few miles beyond the park, on the left side of the road, you'll find Nine Mile County Park (also known affectionately as Nine Mile Swamp), with 20 miles of hiking and cross-country skiing trails.

Farther west on County N, you'll see fields of wooden posts supporting roofs of screen shades. These are ginseng fields planted by Wisconsin's most recent immigrant group, the Hmong people, originally from the mountains of Laos. The Hmong were recruited by the CIA to fight on the side of U.S. troops in the Vietnam War as the fighting spilled over the borders of Vietnam. After the fall of Saigon, the Hmong were persecuted for their role in the war, and many families fled to refugee camps in Thailand before finally making the journey to America. The Hmong have settled in many parts of the U.S., but few places have felt their cultural impact as much as central Wisconsin. The *New York Times* reported in 1990 that up to that time, Marathon County had seen the greatest percentage increase in southeast Asian immigration of any county in the country. In addition to their fields, the Hmong have made an impression with their colorful and intricately embroidered tapestries, which recount their people's history.

Continue west on County N through the gently rolling hills of central Wisconsin. Personally, I think this is some of the most beautiful country to be found anywhere (and I've been around), but then I grew up here, so maybe I'm biased. Roughly 10 miles from Rib Mountain, turn right and head north on Wisconsin Highway 107. One of the reasons so many German and Polish immigrants settled here is that the countryside bears a striking

View from Rib Mountain.

resemblance to the land they left behind. Approximately 3 miles north on WI 107, you come to Marathon City and then cross Wisconsin Highway 29. Continue 15 miles on WI 107 to the junction with Wisconsin Highway 64, and follow WI 107/WI 64 for 9 miles into Merrill.

WI 107/WI 64 is also Merrill's Second Street, and as you roll through downtown, you'll see Merrill's old City Hall, an excellent example of nineteenth-century Richardsonian architecture. The building was completed in 1889 and has since been converted into apartments. The Merrill Historical Museum, open from 1 to 4 P.M. every day, is found 1 block north of the old City Hall on Third Street, housed in the home of Merrill's first mayor, Thomas Blythe Scott. The house was built in 1881, and the museum today features a Victorian parlor and bedroom, as well as displays on the logging era and a blacksmith shop. Continue through downtown and turn left where WI 107 leaves WI 64 and heads north for 3 miles to Council Grounds State Park, the end of this drive.

The park entrance is a left turn. Local legend has it that the Ojibwe used to travel by canoe down the Wisconsin River and gather here for their annual festivals and councils—thus the area became known as Council Grounds. Big Pines Nature Trail takes you through stands of white and Norway pine, hardwoods, and hemlock that escaped the axe during the furious felling of the logging era. The park also has hiking and biking trails, a beach, a picnic area and a fifty-five-site campground. You can do a driving loop through this beautiful park of tall trees. Bear right at the fork at the campground, then bear left toward the beach a bit later; from the beach, the road rolls along the river until turning left back to the park entrance.

This park, like Dells of the Eau Claire County Park at the beginning of this drive, is located on the terminal moraine, the long, winding line of hills left at the farthest extent of the glacier's reach. The glacier pushed and carried huge quantities of boulders, sand, and gravel along its advancing edge. When the glacier stopped its advance and began to melt back, all the material carried at the front was dropped onto the landscape. At Eau Claire Dells, the terminal moraine runs north-south, and here it runs generally east-west, making a 90-degree turn northeast of here in Langlade County.

From here you can follow the terminal moraine west on Drive 24.

24

Chippewa Moraine

Council Grounds State Park to New Auburn

General description: This 100-mile drive runs due west, sometimes cross-ing, sometimes running south of, and sometimes running north of the winding line of hills called the Chippewa moraine, a landform left by the last Ice Age glacier eleven thousand years ago. Starting at Council Grounds State Park north of Merrill, this route mostly runs on a back road called County Highway M, rolling through forests, hills, and tamarack bogs.

Special attractions: Council Grounds State Park, Chequamegon Na-tional Forest, Chippewa Moraine Ice Age Scientific Reserve, camping, hik-ing, biking, wildlife watching, fishing, boating.

Location: North-central Wisconsin.

Drive route numbers: Wisconsin Highways 64 and 107, County High-way M through Lincoln, Taylor and Chippewa Counties.

Travel season: Year-round.

Camping: 55 sites at Council Grounds State Park, 70 sites at Mondeaux Dam Recreation Area, 10 sites at Kathryn Lake National Forest Camp-ground, 78 sites at Chippewa National Forest Campground.

Services: Full services in Merrill, limited elsewhere.

 The drive

This drive starts at Council Grounds State Park on the Wisconsin River 3 miles north of Merrill. To get there from U.S. Highway 51/Interstate High-way 39, take Wisconsin Highway 64 west into Merrill. At the intersection with Business US 51 (the old route of US 51, which ran through Merrill before the new highway was built to bypass the town entirely), you'll see the Lincoln County Courthouse, completed in 1903, and open 8:30 A.M. to 4:30 P.M., Monday through Friday. Designed by Milwaukee architect Henry Van Rhyn, the courthouse features a huge dome and rotunda, as well as historical exhibits inside. Continue on WI 64. Cross the river, turn right onto Wisconsin Highway 107, and travel north 3 miles to Council Grounds State Park—the entrance is on your left. Local legend has it that the Ojibwe used to gather here for their annual festivals and councils after traveling by canoe down the Wisconsin River—thus the name Council Grounds. Big Pines Nature Trail takes you through stands of white and Norway pine, hardwoods, and hemlock that escaped the axe during the furious felling of the logging era. The park also has hiking and biking trails, a beach, a picnic area, and a fifty-five-site campground. You can do a driving loop through this beautiful park of tall trees: bear right at the fork at the campground, then bear left toward the beach a bit later; from the beach the road rolls along the river until turning left back to the park entrance.

The park is also right on the terminal moraine—the long, winding line of hills left at the farthest extent of the glacier's reach. The glacier pushed and carried huge quantities of boulders, sand, and gravel along its advancing edge. When the glacier stopped its advance and began to melt back, all the material carried at the front was dropped onto the landscape—the glacier's gravestone. This drive crosses central Wisconsin east to west in an almost straight line, sometimes running south of the terminal moraine, sometimes crossing it, and sometimes running north of it.

Head back to Merrill on WI 107 and turn right at the stop sign and junction with WI 64 (which is also Merrill's 2nd Street). On 2nd Street in downtown, Merrill's old City Hall is an excellent example of Richardsonian architecture. The building was completed in 1889 and has since been converted into apartments. The Merrill Historical Museum, open from 1 to 4 P.M. every day, is found one block north of the old City Hall on Third Street, housed in the home of Merrill's first mayor, Thomas Blythe Scott. The house was built in 1881, and the museum today features a Victorian parlor and bedroom, as well as displays on the logging era and a replica of a blacksmith shop.

Follow WI 64 west from Merrill. For the approximately 40 miles between Merrill and Wisconsin Highway 13, the route lies south of the terminal moraine of the glacier's Wisconsin Valley Lobe. The glacier did not advance (or retreat) as a single unit. Variations in local topography caused different rates of advancement in different parts (officially called lobes by glaciologists) of the glacier. The Wisconsin Valley Lobe of the glacier was about 70 miles wide, and Merrill sits about halfway between what were its eastern and western borders. It pushed due south, bounded by the Chippewa Lobe to the west and the Langlade Lobe to the east. About 7 miles out of town, continue forward onto Lincoln County Highway M where WI 64 takes a big left turn and heads south. For the first few miles on this stretch, you'll see a mixture of fields and forests, but the farms soon end and you roll through uninterrupted trees. Mostly, the land is a glacial outwash plain, swept clean and flat by the raging meltwaters. After crossing into Taylor County, the trees give way to farms on the south side of the road, and the forests on both sides of the road are interrupted by shrubby, bushy wetlands.

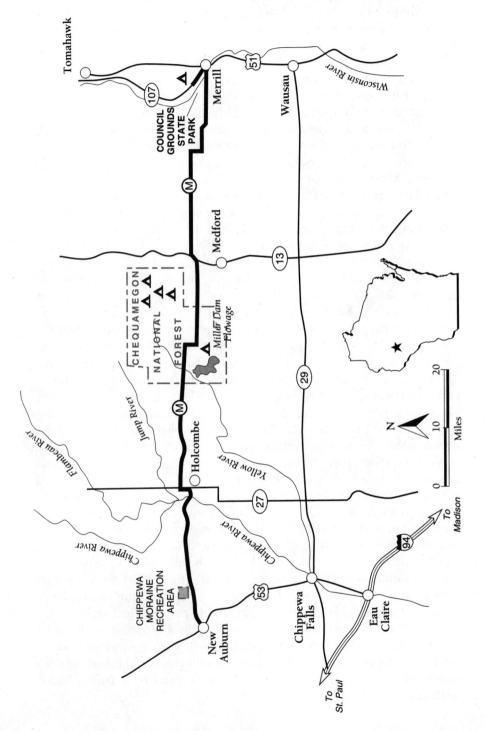

Drive 24: Chippewa Moraine

Council Grounds State Park to New Auburn

At the junction with WI 13, you'll cross the terminal moraine of the Chippewa Lobe of the glacier. The Chippewa Lobe pushed farther south than the Wisconsin Valley Lobe because the Wisconsin Valley Lobe was impeded by highlands, the remnants of an ancient mountain range, due north of Merrill (Drive 7 wanders through the Northern Highland State Forest). These hills gave the Wisconsin Valley Lobe more trouble than the flatter land west did the Chippewa Lobe, and thus the Chippewa Lobe reached farther south.

Drive 1 mile south on WI 13, then turn right at the sign to the national forest campground to continue on County M. You're now traveling north of the terminal moraine, with some hills rising between large, flat tamarack bogs and stands of birch, aspen, white pine, and hardwoods. A right turn onto Taylor County Highway E, approximately 7 miles from WI 13, will take you to the Mondeaux Dam Recreation Area, which offers great fishing and boating and 70 campsites in 5 campgrounds. You'll also find a segment of the Ice Age Trail, the 1,000-mile hiking trail that follows the different glacial moraines across the state, along the shores of the Mondeaux Flowage.

About 2 miles west of County E you enter the Chequamegon National Forest, and you'll find it hillier than the land east of here. Near Perkinstown, approximately 7 miles from the National Forest border, a left onto Forest Road 121 in Perkinstown will take you to the 10-site national forest campground on 62-acre Kathryn Lake, 0.5 mile from County M. The road turns north briefly, then west again. About 7 miles from Perkinstown, a right onto Forest Road 1417 leads to the 78-site Chippewa National Forest Campground, 1 mile south of County M. Sitting on the eastern shore of the 2,714-acre Miller Dam Flowage, the campground has two beaches, a playground, and hot showers. Continue on County M. You'll soon cross the Yellow River, which, when blocked by Miller Dam, backed up to form the Miller Dam Flowage. A few miles beyond the Yellow River, you leave the national forest.

At the intersection with Wisconsin Highway 73, turn right and follow County M/WI 73 north 1 mile into the bustling hamlet of Hannibal. Turn left to continue on County M. Travel west approximately 15 miles to the junction with Wisconsin Highway 27 and turn left. Take County M/WI 27 south 1 mile into Holcombe, and turn right to continue on County M. Just outside of Holcombe you cross the Holcombe Flowage of the Chippewa River and enter the Chippewa County Forest. You'll notice that it's distinctly hillier in the county forest—you're back at the terminal moraine. The hills of the moraine run generally north-south here; the Chippewa Lobe made its farthest push southward a few miles to the southeast. You'll also notice an abundance of what geologists call kettle lakes. As the glacier melted and its front edge receded northward, huge blocks of ice fell from the glacial front and were buried in sand deposited by meltwater streams. As the ice blocks

The Yellow River in the Chequamegon National Forest.

slowly melted, the sand and rocks above them slowly sank, eventually leaving these kettles, some of which filled with water.

Soon after you leave the Chippewa County Forest you come upon the Chippewa Moraine Ice Age Scientific Reserve Visitors Center, which offers spectacular vistas from atop one of the moraine's hills. Signs placed outside the visitors center interpret the glacial features visible from the hill top, and inside the visitors center you'll find displays on glacial landforms and history, reptiles for the kids to play with, and other hands-on exhibits. The reserve also has 23 miles of excellent hiking—the visitors center has trail maps and information. Currently, only rustic backpack camping is allowed along the trails.

County M continues west through the white-pine lined kettle lakes to the intersection with U.S. Highway 53, the end of this drive.

Appendix

Sources of more information

For more information on lands and events, please contact the following agencies and organizations.

Drive 1

Kettle Moraine State Forest,
  North Unit
1765 County Highway G North
Campbellsport, WI 53010
414-533-8322

Kettle Moraine State Forest,
  South Unit
South 91 West
39091 Highway 59
Eagle, WI 53119
414-594-6200

Pike Lake State Park
3340 Kettle Moraine Road
Hartford, WI 53027
414-673-7999

Holy Hill National Shrine of Mary
1525 Carmel Road
Hubertus, WI 53033
414-628-1838

Drive 2

Kewaunee Chamber of Commerce
P.O. Box 243
Kewaunee, WI 54216-0243
1-800-666-8214/414-388-4822

Kohler-Andrae State Park
1520 Old Park Road
Sheboygan, WI 53081
414-452-3457

Point Beach State Forest
9400 County Highway O
Two Rivers, WI 54241
414-794-7480

Sheboygan County Convention and
  Visitors Bureau
712 Riverfront Drive, Suite 101
Sheboygan, WI 53081-4665
1-800-457-9497/414-457-9495

Manitowoc Visitor & Convention
  Bureau
P.O. Box 966
Manitowoc, WI 54221
414-683-4388

Drive 3

Green Bay Visitor & Convention
  Bureau
1901 South Oneida Street
P.O. Box 10596
Green Bay, WI 54307-0596
1-800-236-EXPO/414-494-9507

Green Bay Packer Hall of Fame
855 Lombardi Avenue
P.O. Box 10567
Green Bay, WI 54307-0567
414-499-4281

Rock Island State Park
Washington Island, WI 54246
414-854-2500

Peninsula State Park
P.O. Box 218
Fish Creek, WI 54212

Door County Chamber of Commerce
P.O. Box 406
Sturgeon Bay, WI 54235
1-800-52-RELAX/414-743-4456

Newport State Park
475 County Highway NP
Ellison Bay, WI 54210
414-854-2500

Whitefish Dunes State Park
3701 Clark Lake Road
Sturgeon Bay, WI 54235
414-823-2400

Washington Island Ferry Line
    Northport Pier
Highway 42 & Death's Door
Washington Island, WI 54246
1-800-223-2094/414/847-2546

Drive 4

Waupaca Area Chamber of
    Commerce
221 South Main Street
Box 262
Waupaca, WI 54981-0262
1-800-236-2222/715-258-7343

Oconto County Forestry
    & Park Agent
300 Washington Street
Oconto, WI 54153
414-834-6820

Copper Culture Mound State Park
Mill Road, P.O. Box 168
Oconto, WI 54153
414-834-3363

Menominee Logging Museum
P.O. Box 910
Keshena, WI 54135
715-799-3757

Drive 5

Peshtigo Chamber of Commerce
P.O. Box 36
Peshtigo, WI 54157-0036
715-582-3041

Marinette Chamber of Commerce
601 Marinette Avenue
P.O. Box 512
Marinette, WI 54143-0512
1-800-236-6681/715-735-6681

Florence County Visitor Center
HC1, Box 82
Florence, WI 54121
715-528-5377

Drive 6

Lakewood Ranger District
15805 State Road 32
Lakewood, WI 54138
715-276-3909

Drive 7

Northern Highland State Forest
4125 County Highway M
Boulder Junction, WI 54512
715-385-2727

Rhinelander Chamber of Commerce
135 South Stevens Street
P.O. Box 795
Rhinelander, WI 54501-0795
1-800-236-4386/715-362-7464

Lac du Flambeau Chippewa Museum
County Highway D, Downtown
Lac du Flambeau, WI 54538
715-588-3333

Minoqua Chamber of Commerce
8216 Highway 51 South
P.O. Box 1006-W
Minoqua, WI 54548-1006
1-800-446-6748/715-356-5266

Drive 8

Hurley Chamber of Commerce
110 Iron Street
Hurley, WI 54534
715-561-4334

Copper Falls State Park
Route 1, Box 17 AA
Mellen, WI 54546
715-274-5123

Drive 9

Chequamegon National Forest
1170 Fourth Avenue South
Park Falls, WI 54552
715-762-2461

Hayward Area Chamber of
  Commerce
101 West First Street
P.O. Box 726
Hayward, WI 54803-0726
1-800-826-3474/715-634-8662

Drive 10

Apostle Islands National Lakeshore
Route 1, Box 4
Old Courthouse Bldg.
Bayfield, WI 54814
715-779-3397

Amnicon Falls State Park
6294 South State Road 35
Superior, WI 54880-8326
715-399-8073 (winter)
715-398-3000 (summer)

Brule River State Forest
Box 125
Brule, WI 54820-0125
715-372-4866

Bad River Tribal Center
Highway 2
Odonah, WI 54861
715-682-4134

Big Bay State Park
P.O. Box 589
Bayfield, WI 54814
715-779-3346 (winter)
715-747-6425 (summer)

Bayfield County Tourism &
  Recreation
117 East Sixth Street
Box 832 W
Washburn, WI 54891-0832
1-800-472-6338/715-373-6125

Pattison State Park
6294 South State Road 35
Superior, WI 54880-8326
715-399-8073 (winter)
715-398-3000 (summer)

Red Cliff Chamber of Commerce
P.O. Box 1350
Bayfield, WI 54814
715-779-5225

Madeline Island Ferry Line
Washington Avenue
Bayfield, WI 54814
715-747-2051

Superior Convention & Visitors
Bureau
305 Harbor View Parkway
Superior, WI 54880
1-800-942-5313/715-392-2773

Ashland Chamber of Commerce
320 West Fourth Street
Ashland, WI 54806-0746
1-800-284-9484/715-682-2500

Drive 11

Hayward Area Chamber of
Commerce
101 West First Street
P.O. Box 726
Hayward, WI 54803-0726
1-800-826-3474/715-634-8662

Cable Area Chamber of Commerce
P.O. Box 217
Cable, WI 54821-0217
1-800-533-7454/715-798-3833

St. Croix National Scenic Riverway
P.O. Box 708
St. Croix Falls, WI 54024
715-483-3284

Chequamegon National Forest
1170 Fourth Avenue South
Park Falls, WI 54552
715-762-2461

Drive 12

Prescott Welcome & Heritage Center
233 Broad Street North
Prescott, WI 54021
1-800-4-PIERCE/715-262-4800

Kinnickinnic State Park
11983 820th Avenue West
River Falls, WI 54022
715-425-1129

St. Croix National Scenic Riverway
P.O. Box 708
St. Croix Falls, WI 54024
715-483-3284

Hudson Chamber of Commerce
421 Second Street
P.O. Box 438
Hudson, WI 54016-0438
1-800-657-6775/715-386-8411

Interstate Park & Ice Age
Interpretive Center
Highway 35, Box 703
St. Croix Falls, WI 54024
715-483-3747

Governor Knowles State Forest
Box 367
Grantsburg, WI 54840
715-463-2898

Drive 13

Prescott Welcome & Heritage Center
233 Broad Street North
Prescott, WI 54021
1-800-4-PIERCE/715-262-4800

Perrot State Park
Route 1, Box 407
Trempealeau, WI 54661
608-534-6409

Trempealeau National Wildlife
Refuge
Route 1, Box 1602
Trempealeau, WI 54661

Trempealeau Chamber of Commerce
P.O. Box 212
Trempealeau, WI 54661-0212
608-534-6780

La Crosse Convention & Visitors
Bureau
410 East Veterans Memorial Drive
La Crosse, WI 54602-1895
608-784-4880

Drive 14

Willow River State Park
1034 County Highway A
Hudson, WI 54016
715-386-5931

Hoffman Hills Recreation Area
Brickyard Road
Route 6, Box 1
Menomonie, WI 54751
715-232-2631

Eau Claire Convention & Visitors
Bureau
2127 Brackett Avenue
Eau Claire, WI 54701
1-800-344-FUNN/715-831-2345

Black River Falls Area Chamber of
Commerce
336 North Water Street
Black River Falls, WI 54615
1-800-404-4008/715-284-4658

Drive 15

Trempealeau Chamber of Commerce
P.O. Box 212
Trempealeau, WI 54661-0212
608-534-6780

Black River Falls Area Chamber of
Commerce
336 North Water Street
Black River Falls, WI 54615
1-800-404-4008/715-284-4658

Trempealeau County Clerk's Office
1720 Main Street
P.O. Box 67
Whitehall, WI 54773-0067
715-538-2311

Drive 16

La Crosse Convention & Visitors
Bureau
410 East Veterans Memorial Drive
La Crosse, WI 54602-1895
608-784-4880

Blackhawk Park
Route 1
De Soto, WI 54624

Prairie du Chien Chamber of
Commerce
211 South Main Street
P.O. Box 326
Prairie du Chien, WI 53821-1673
1-800-PDC-1673

Wyalusing State Park
13342 County Highway C
Bagley, WI 53801
608-996-2261

Drive 17

Wyalusing State Park
13342 County Highway C
Bagley, WI 53801
608-996-2261

Kickapoo Indian Caverns
West 200 Rhein Hollow Road
Wauzeka, WI 53826
608-875-7723

Natural Bridge State Park
South 5975 Park Road
Baraboo, WI 53913
608-356-8301

Richland Center Chamber of
  Commerce
170 West Seminary
P.O. Box 128
Richland Center, WI 53581-1398
608-647-6205

Spring Green Chamber of Commerce
P.O. Box 3
Spring Green, WI 53588-0351
608-588-2042

Sauk Prairie Area Chamber of
  Commerce
213 Water Street
Sauk City, WI 53583
608-643-4168

Drive 18

New Glarus Woods State Park
N3150 Highway 81
Box 256
Monroe, WI 53566
608-325-4844/ 608-527-2335

New Glarus Tourism & Chamber
  of Commerce
P.O. Box 713
New Glarus, WI 53574-0713
608-527-2095

Mineral Point Chamber of
  Commerce
237 High Street
Box 78
Mineral Point, WI 53565-0078
608-987-3201

Platteville Chamber of Commerce
275 Highway 151 West
Platteville, WI 53818
608-348-8888

Browntown-Cadiz Springs Park
North 3140 Highway 81
Box 256
Monroe, WI 53566
608-325-4844/608-966-3777

Yellowstone Lake State Park
7896 Lake Road
Blanchardville, WI 53516-9321
608-523-4427

Drive 19

Janesville Chamber of Commerce
20 South Main Street
P.O. Box 8008
Janesville, WI 53547-8008
608-757-3160

Devil's Lake State Park
South 5975 Park Road
Baraboo, WI 53913
608-356-8301/608-356-6618 for
campsite info

Baraboo Chamber of Commerce
P.O. Box 442
Baraboo, WI 53913-0442
1-800-BARABOO/608-356-8333

Mount Horeb Chamber of Commerce
P.O. Box 84
Mount Horeb, WI 53572-0084
608-437-5914

Blue Mound State Park
4350 Mounds Park Road
P.O. Box 98
Blue Mounds, WI 53517
608-437-5711

Drive 20

Portage Chamber of Commerce
301 West Wisconsin
Portage, WI 53901
1-800-474-2525/608-742-6242

Wisconsin Dells Visitors Bureau
701 Superior Street
Box 390
Wisconsin Dells, WI 53965
1-800-22-DELLS/608-254-4636

Rocky Arbor State Park
East 10320 Fern Dell Road
Baraboo, WI 53913
608-254-2333 (winter)
608-254-8001 (summer)

Mirror Lake State Park
East 10320 Fern Dell Road
Baraboo, WI 53913
608-254-2333

Tomah Chamber of Commerce
708 South Superior Ave.
P.O. Box 625
Tomah, WI 54660-0625
1-800-368-3601/608-372-2166

Mill Bluff State Park
Box 99
Mill Bluff, WI 54651
608-337-4775 (winter)
608-427-6692 (summer)

Black River State Forest
910 Highway 54 East
Black River Falls, WI 54615
715-284-1400/715-284-4103

Drive 21

Necedah National Wildlife Refuge
Star Route West
Necedah, WI 54646
608-565-2551

Necedah Chamber of Commerce
P.O. Box 345
Necedah, WI 54646-0345
608-565-2260

Roche A Cri State Park
1767 Highway 13 North
Friendship, WI 53934
608-399-6881

Drive 22

Black River State Forest
910 Highway 54 East
Black River Falls, WI 54615
715-284-1400/715-284-4103

Hartman Creek State Park
North 2480 Hartman Creek Road
Waupaca, WI 54981-9727
715-258-2372

Wisconsin Rapids Area Chamber
of Commerce
1120 Lincoln Street
Box 996
Wisconsin Rapids, WI 54495
1-800-554-4484/715-423-1830

Waupaca Area Chamber of
Commerce
221 South Main Street
Box 262
Waupaca, WI 54981-0262
1-800-236-2222/715-258-7343

Black River Falls Chamber of
Commerce
336 North Water Street
Black River Falls, WI 54615
1-800-404-4008/715-284-4658

Chippewa Moraine Recreational Area
13394 County Highway M
New Auburn, Wisconsin 54757
715-967-2800

Chequamegon National Forest
Medford Ranger District
850 North Highway 13
Medford, WI 54451
715-748-4875

Drive 23

Wausau Area Chamber of Commerce
300 Third Street
P.O. Box 6190
Wausau, WI 54402-6190
715-845-6231

Rib Mountain State Park
5301 Rib Mountain Drive
Wausau, Wisconsin 54401
715-359-4522 (winter)
715-842-2522 (summer)

Drive 24

Council Grounds State Park
1110 East 10th Street
Merril, WI 54452
715-536-8773 (winter)
715-536-4502 (summer)

Suggested Reading

Robert E. Gard and L.G. Sorden, *Wisconsin Lore*. Ashland, Wisconsin: Heartland Press, 1962.

Rhoda R. Gilman, *Historic Chequamegon* (a pamphlet). La Pointe, Wisconsin: 1971.

Robert P. Sharp, *Living Ice: Understanding Glaciers and Glaciation*. Cambridge: Cambridge University Press, 1988.

Clark S. Matteson, *An Illustrated History of Wisconsin*. Milwaukee: The Wisconsin Historical Publishing Company, 1893.

U.S. Department of Agriculture, Nicolet National Forest, *Lakewood Auto Tour* (a pamplet).

Don Davenport, editor, *Wisconsin Auto Tours*. Milwaukee: Wisconsin Department of Tourism, 1996.

Index

About the Author

The author and Subie. You may notice Subie's broken nose. Of the incident, Subie says: "The guy in front of me wasn't going fast enough, so I had to hit him. I hope he learned his lesson."

Aaron Cieslicki was born in Superior and grew up in Rothschild, just south of Wausau. His formative years were largly spent causing mischief. After earning degrees in philosophy and linguistics at Macalester College in St. Paul, Minnesota, he began to write freelance articles for magazines and held a variety of jobs to pay the rent. Among other things, he has worked as a disc jockey, stage manager, envelope stuffer, executive waterboy, hardware store clerk, dishwasher, airport security screener, telemarketer, telephone interviewer, tutor, rubber stamper, sports announcer, waiter, word processor, and construction worker/demolisher. He currently lives and works in the twin cities of Minneapolis and St. Paul.

Aaron inherited "the wanderlust" from his mother, for whom no summer was complete without a road trip. He has traveled much of the United States by car, and has traveled to Europe, the Middle East, and the Caribbean as well.